S.E.
Hinton

Other titles in the *Authors Teens Love* series:

Ray Bradbury
*Master of Science Fiction
and Fantasy*
ISBN-13: 978-0-7660-2240-9
ISBN-10:　　0-7660-2240-4

Gary Paulsen
*Voice of Adventure
and Survival*
ISBN-13: 978-0-7660-2721-3
ISBN-10:　　0-7660-2721-X

Orson Scott Card
Architect of Alternate Worlds
ISBN-13: 978-0-7660-2354-3
ISBN-10:　　0-7660-2354-0

Philip Pullman
Master of Fantasy
ISBN-13: 978-0-7660-2447-2
ISBN-10:　　0-7660-2447-4

Roald Dahl
Author of Charlie and the
Chocolate Factory
ISBN-13: 978-0-7660-2353-6
ISBN-10:　　0-7660-2353-2

Jerry Spinelli
Master Teller of Teen Tales
ISBN-13: 978-0-7660-2718-3
ISBN-10:　　0-7660-2718-X

Paula Danziger
Voice of Teen Troubles
ISBN-13: 978-0-7660-2444-1
ISBN-10:　　0-7660-2444-X

R. L. Stine
*Creator of Creepy and
Spooky Stories*
ISBN-13: 978-0-7660-2445-8
ISBN-10:　　0-7660-2445-8

C. S. Lewis
Chronicler of Narnia
ISBN-13: 978-0-7660-2446-5
ISBN-10:　　0-7660-2446-6

J. R. R. Tolkien
Master of Imaginary Worlds
ISBN-13: 978-0-7660-2246-1
ISBN-10:　　0-7660-2246-3

Joan Lowery Nixon
Masterful Mystery Writer
ISBN-13: 978-0-7660-2194-5
ISBN-10:　　0-7660-2194-7

E. B. White
Spinner of Webs and Tales
ISBN-13: 978-0-7660-2350-5
ISBN-10:　　0-7660-2350-8

AUTHORS TEENS LOVE

S.E. Hinton

Author of The Outsiders

Marylou Morano Kjelle

Enslow Publishers, Inc.
40 Industrial Road
Box 398
Berkeley Heights, NJ 07922
USA
http://www.enslow.com

Library of Congress Cataloging-in-Publication Data

Kjelle, Marylou Morano.
    S.E. Hinton : author of *The Outsiders* / Marylou Morano Kjelle.
       p. cm. — (Authors teens love)
    Includes bibliographical references and index.
    ISBN-13: 978-0-7660-2720-6
    ISBN-10: 0-7660-2720-1
    1. Hinton, S. E.—Juvenile literature. 2. Young adult fiction—Authorship—Juvenile literature. 3. Authors, American—20th century—Biography—Juvenile literature. I. Title.
    PS3558.I548Z87 2007
    813'.54—dc22

                2006036820

Printed in the United States of America

10 9 8 7 6 5 4 3 2 1

To Our Readers: We have done our best to make sure all Internet Addresses in this book were active and appropriate when we went to press. However, the author and publisher have no control over and assume no liability for the material available on those Internet sites or on other Web sites they may link to. Any comments or suggestions can be sent by e-mail to comments@enslow.com or to the address on the back cover.

Illustration Credits: All interior images courtesy of the Everett Collection, Inc.; except p. 6, courtesy of Getty Images; p. 20, courtesy of Will Rogers High School; and p. 82, courtesy of AP/Wide World photos.

Cover Illustrations: AP/World Wide Photos (inset portrait) and Carl Feryok (background art).

Contents

Chapter 1

"The Voice of the Youth"

Readers introduced to *The Outsiders* for the first time are often pleasantly surprised to learn two things about its author: S.E. Hinton is a woman, and she was only fifteen years old when she began writing the book.

In 1965, when she was a high school sophomore, Susan Hinton, a voracious reader, became disheartened by the themes of puppy love, first dates, and Mary-Jane-goes-to-the-prom that dominated the adolescent fiction popular at the time.[1] To Hinton, such anxieties were not very realistic, nor were they the most important concerns in the lives of the teens she knew, who wrestled daily with issues of peer pressure, gangs, violence, drugs, and abusive parents.

Hinton wanted to see young adult fiction books

embrace teenage reality. She also believed that stories centered on true teenage concerns would best be told, and therefore written, from a teenager's point of view. In her experience, adult authors wrote about teenage issues either from their own memories or from a fear of getting too close to real teenage concerns. "Teenagers today want to read about teenagers today. The world is changing, yet the authors of books for teenagers are still 15 years behind the times," Hinton wrote after the publication of *The Outsiders*.[2]

Intent on writing a true-life story about teenagers, Hinton began working on a book, not for publication, but for herself. She wrote of teenage life as she knew it at Will Rogers High School, the large school she attended in Tulsa, Oklahoma. There the students were divided into many groups, but the two extremes were the "greasers," who came from working-class families, and the "Socs" (pronounced "soshes," for Socials), whose parents made up Tulsa's upper class.[3] The two groups abhorred each other and their loathing often resulted in violence. This social division and hatred between the two groups deeply concerned Hinton, a fiercely independent nonconformist who, being neither a greaser nor a "Soc," found herself outside of both groups.[4]

The book Hinton began in 1965 became *The Outsiders*, a critically acclaimed fictional story of the conflicts between Tulsa teenagers who belong to different social classes. The novel is written from the point of view of an outsider, Ponyboy

Curtis, an orphaned fourteen-year-old greaser being raised by his older brothers, Darry and Sodapop. The book, which begins and ends with the same words, is an English class composition assignment that Ponyboy must complete. As the plot of *The Outsiders* unfolds in Ponyboy's own words, the rivalry between the greasers and the Socs erupts in violence, hostility, and brutality.

"Nobody worries about the prom in *The Outsiders*; they're more concerned with just staying alive until June," wrote Jay Daly in his critical study, *Presenting S.E. Hinton*.[5]

Hinton wrote four drafts of *The Outsiders* before she was ready to pursue publication. During her junior year in high school, when she wrote and revised the majority of the novel, Hinton received a grade of "D" in creative writing, a story she relates as often as she can. ". . . I was writing my book and not doing my class work," she remembers.[6] Everyday school assignments did not interest Hinton, who was working on a novel.

Hinton gave the completed manuscript of *The Outsiders* to a friend's mother who was a published children's book author. She read it and then gave it to another author. That author suggested Hinton get in touch with her New York City agent, who was from Curtis Brown, Ltd., a well-established literary agency. At age seventeen, Hinton had not known there was such a thing as an agent. With the agent's help, *The Outsiders* was sold to Viking Press, the second publisher it was offered to. The book was released in the spring of 1967, when Hinton was a freshman at the University of Tulsa.

Since the protagonist of *The Outsiders* is a boy, Hinton's editor at Viking Press suggested she write under the genderless pen name "S.E. Hinton" instead of her given name, Susan Eloise Hinton. The publisher was concerned that readers would think less of the book if they knew that its strong, male point of view had been written by a woman.[7] On this point, Hinton agreed. "I figured that most boys would look at the book and think, 'What can a chick know about stuff like that?'" said Hinton.[8] Therefore, it did not surprise her when, after *The Outsiders* was published, she began receiving letters from readers addressed to "Mr. Hinton." Even reviewers were fooled by her pen name. "[T]he author's skirts didn't hang in the story . . . In retrospect, the obvious clue is that maybe only a girl could [show] . . . the soft centers of these boys and how often they do give way to tears," wrote a reviewer in *School Library Journal*.[9]

Hinton's authentic portrayal of teenage gangs was a subject not previously explored in a young adult novel. Soon after *The Outsiders* was published, it was evident that Hinton had written a story that teens could relate to.[10] Although it was not an overnight success, the book slowly gained popularity among teenagers. "It built gradually, from teachers telling teachers and kids telling kids," said Hinton.[11]

Now credited with transforming the genre of teenage fiction and revolutionizing writing for

The young star-filled cast of the 1983 film adaptation of S.E. Hinton's *The Outsiders* (clockwise, from far left): Emilio Estevez, Patrick Swayze, Matt Dillon, Rob Lowe, Tom Cruise, C. Thomas Howell, and Ralph Macchio.

young adults, *The Outsiders* was not at first widely accepted either by reviewers or educators. Its scenes of violence and ruthlessness have caused *The Outsiders* to be banned by several schools in the United States. One reviewer objected to the book's cruelty, stating that it mythologized the tragic beauty of violent youth. "The vast majority of teenagers personally experience nothing close to the violence of Hinton's characters, nor do they suffer the [loss] of parental supervision of her Peter Pan-like cast of orphans and near orphans who must look after themselves or watch out that alcoholic, abusive parents do not do them harm," wrote Michael Malone in *Nation* magazine.[12]

> **Hinton's authentic portrayal of teenage gangs was a subject not previously explored in a young adult novel.**

Hinton countered the objection to her writing by explaining that violence is a part of the lives of teenagers. Teens see violence on television and in the movies, and they get into fights at the local drive-in. Things like this are going to take place as long as there are kids, she answered in an article for the *New York Times Book Review*.[13] Parents also had concerns about *The Outsiders*; many believed that teens who read the book would be encouraged to idolize a life of lawlessness and destruction.[14]

Reviews are just certain people's opinions. Sometimes the very things one reviewer likes about a book are the same things another reviewer dislikes. Therefore, while some reviewers objected to *The Outsiders*, others applauded the book for its vision. Thomas Fleming, writing in the *New York Times*, praised Hinton. "Miss Hinton's performance is impressive. . . . She has produced a book alive with the fresh dialogue of her contemporaries, and has wound around it a story that captures . . . a rather unnerving slice of teenage America," he wrote.[15] Another reviewer called *The Outsiders* "a remarkable novel . . . a moving, credible view of *The Outsiders* from the inside."[16]

Regardless of what reviewers wrote, Hinton found the responses from young readers especially gratifying. Teenagers from every part of the country wrote to Hinton to tell her how true-to-life they found *The Outsiders*, and how thankful they were to find in Hinton an author who was able to express how they felt about issues that were important to them. In writing a book for herself, one that she wanted to read, Hinton had unknowingly written for thousands of other young people who were also looking for reading material with the same graphic portrayal of realism.

Hinton's approach to teenage fiction earned her the title "The Voice of the Youth." However, publishing a book that would change the way authors wrote teenage fiction was not uppermost in her mind when she wrote *The Outsiders*. "I just wanted to write something that dealt with what I saw kids really doing," Hinton explained.[17]

By all rights, S.E. Hinton should have been one of the intended readers of *The Outsiders*, not its author.[18] It was Hinton's real-life perspective of teenage issues, however, that revolutionized writing for young adults. With more than fourteen million copies sold (400,000 in 2004 alone), *The Outsiders* is the best-selling young adult novel of all time. Its popularity among teenage readers was the impetus for an entire generation of authors who wrote about real characters and their true-to-life situations for a teenage audience.

Chapter 2

"A Teenage Wonder"

No one is really quite sure of the actual date of Susan Eloise Hinton's birth. No one, that is, except Hinton herself. Supposedly she was born on July 22, 1950, but some sources list her birthday as one or two years earlier. Hinton will not say exactly how old she is.[1] The mystery arises from the fact that the author was so young when she published her first book that her editor at Viking Press added a year or two to her age to give her more credibility. "I began the first draft of *The Outsiders* when I was fifteen. Nobody believes that, so I usually say sixteen. My editors say seventeen, just in case," explains Hinton.[2]

There is no confusion as to the place of Hinton's birth, however. She was born and raised in Tulsa, Oklahoma, and it is the place she still calls home. Throughout her life, Hinton has spent very little time away from Tulsa. "I grew up here and my friends are here. There's nothing wrong here," says Hinton about her birthplace and home.[3]

Tulsa lies in northeastern Oklahoma, in the part of the state that borders Kansas, Missouri, and Arkansas. Oil was discovered in Tulsa and the surrounding areas in the early 1900s. The city was still feeling the effects of this discovery when Hinton was growing up in the 1950s and 1960s. Calling itself the "Oil Capital of the World," mid-twentieth century Tulsa was a mix of people of

The discovery of oil brought "new money" into Tulsa and divided the city.

different socioeconomic classes. Many of those living there at the time had American Indian roots and were descendents of Choctaw, Creek, and Chickasaw tribes. Others traced their ancestry to the Cherokee clans that had been forcibly removed from Georgia and traveled the "Trail of Tears" into Oklahoma during the winter of 1838–1839.

The discovery of oil brought "new money" into Tulsa and divided the city into neighborhoods almost as neatly as does the Arkansas River, which runs through its center. The rich gravitated to the residential southern and eastern sides of Tulsa, where they built large homes with their newfound wealth. The less-well-off working- and middle-class families lived in north and west Tulsa. Most of these residents worked at blue-collar jobs in the west Tulsa oil refineries, located along the Arkansas River, and at McDonnell Douglas and American Airlines in north Tulsa.[4]

Hinton, who is called Susie by her family and friends, grew up in a working-class neighborhood in Tulsa's north side. Her father, Grady Hinton, was a door-to-door salesman, and her mother, Lillian, worked on an assembly line. Hinton has one sister, Beverly, who is two years younger. The family attended a "fundamentalist, hellfire and brimstone" church and, as a result, Hinton lost interest in religion at an early age.[5]

Hinton is a very private person, and for many years she did not talk much about her childhood except to say that it was "normal" and included aunts, uncles, grandparents, and pets, in addition to her immediate family.[6] She was a tomboy whose close friends were mostly boys, with whom she played football and hunted. She also spent time at her grandmother's farm, where she passed many hours riding her aunt's horse. Hinton recalls feeling "as one with a horse"[7] and she dreamed of the day when she could afford to buy her own. At one time Hinton thought that if she did not become a writer, she would become a cowboy.[8]

Recently Hinton revealed that her childhood was not as pleasant as she had previously indicated. In September 2005, she told a reporter for the

New York Times that her father was a cold and unaffectionate man, and that her mother was physically and emotionally abusive.[9] Perhaps as a way of escaping what was at times an unpleasant family situation, Hinton developed a love of reading at an early age. She read "everything, including Comet cans and coffee labels." When it came to fiction, cowboy and horse stories were what she preferred.[10] The first book she remembers taking out of the library was *Peanuts the Pony*.[11] As a child, Hinton was quiet and shy, and reading, for her, took the place of friends. To Hinton, reading a book was not merely reading a book: it was having a conversation with the author.[12]

> **She read "everything, including Comet cans and coffee labels."**

Hinton knew she wanted to be a writer by the time she was in third grade. The first things she wrote were notes in her journal and poetry. She taught herself to type when she was around twelve years old and shortly thereafter began composing stories. She started to write, in part, so that she could have something to read.[13] She had read all the horse books that she could find, and she did not feel she was ready to start reading adult books. The plots of the sugarcoated novels about prom queens and football heroes that other girls her age were reading did not seem real to her. So Hinton began to write her own stories about cowboys and horses. Usually her stories were told from a boy's point of view. By the time she wrote *The Outsiders*, Hinton had already written two unpublished novels about horses and cowboys. Later, when *The Outsiders* was released, she called it "my third first book."[14]

Today Hinton credits her childhood love of reading for teaching her how to be a good writer. She learned how to create sentences, paragraphs, and chapters by studying the way other authors wrote. However, she admits, reading did not help her build her spelling skills.[15] (This is a task she happily leaves to her editor when she writes today.)

Hinton's home was not a literary home,[16] and Lillian especially did not share her daughter's passion for writing. "When I was writing she'd come into my room, grab my hair and throw me in front of the TV," Hinton remembers.[17] Once Lillian threw Hinton's manuscripts into the trash burner but later allowed her to retrieve them.[18] Hinton kept telling herself things would get better.[19] Soon after *The Outsiders* was published, Lillian read the novel for the first time. "Susie, where did you pick up all of this?" Lillian asked her daughter in amazement.[20]

The mid-1960s, the years Hinton attended Will Rogers High School, were intense times for America. Far-reaching political and social upheavals were being felt throughout the United States. The country was still dealing with the effects of sweeping

Civil Rights legislation that had been enacted a decade earlier. Also, America was involved in a war in a small southeast Asian country. Vietnam was a place most Americans had never heard of before the war. College students and others held "sit-ins" to protest the war and other government policies. Some of those who protested were called "hippies" and were accused of being un-American.

The sixties were also years of great strides for American women. The economic, reproductive, and social differences between men and women were being recognized and challenged. Feminism, which was also known as the women's liberation movement, and called "women's lib" for short, was gaining momentum across the country. It was changing family dynamics everywhere.

The students attending Will Rogers High School in the 1960s were aware of what was happening outside of the city of Tulsa and their state of Oklahoma. But most students were not affected. Will Rogers students stayed focused on their studies, their social lives, and their afterschool activities. Most of the girls took dance lessons at Skilly's School

S.E. Hinton's senior portrait from her high school yearbook.

of Ballroom Dancing located in the city at 15th and Peoria and belonged to one of two dance sororities: the Damsels or the Highlanders. The boys had their own social club called the Vikings and participated in sports during Sixth Hour Gym. Some of the boys belonged to the Order of DeMolay,[21] an international Masonic organization devoted to teaching leadership skills to teenage boys. There were students with other interests as well; some were involved with the Student Council and others were into arts and crafts.

Hinton did not join many clubs in high school, but she did have friends, mostly boys. She had grown up around boys and felt more comfortable around them than she did around girls.[22] There were not many opportunities for girls in those days. "[G]irls were mainly concerned with getting their hair done and lining their eyes. It was such a passive society. Girls got their status from their boyfriends. They weren't interested in doing anything on their own. I didn't know what they were talking about," remembers Hinton.[23] She found nothing in the female culture to identify with,[24] and her fellow classmates saw her as being a little eccentric.[25] Instead of an active social life, Hinton kept busy with her part-time jobs of working in a bookstore and running an elevator. And there was always reading and writing to keep her occupied.

Although she did not realize it at the time, Hinton's identification with boys would have a major impact on her writing. It is what allowed her to tell her stories from a male point of view and develop the personalities of her male characters.

Despite the many groups of students at Will Rogers High School, the two that stood out most were the greasers, who came from working-class families, and the "Socs" whose parents made up Tulsa's upper class. The greasers wore black leather jackets, walked around with cigarettes dangling from their lips, and slicked their hair straight back. The Socs wore madras shirts and drove Mustangs and Corvairs. Hinton lived in a greaser neighborhood, but in school she was placed in Soc classrooms.[26] She was friends with members of both groups but belonged to neither.

Hinton was irritated by the way the different groups at school treated one another based on the way they dressed or their economic background.[27] She felt she was the only person questioning the fact that "you got stuck in your group and that was where you were."[28] She remembers that "The custom . . . of driving by a shabby boy and screaming 'Greaser!' at him always made me boil."[29] Hinton had not even realized that the kids she spent time with were greasers until she heard the Socs taunting them. Hinton could hold her own when she was out with the greasers, and her experiences with them contributed to what she calls a "very interesting adolescence." Hinton joined in greaser fights and was chased by the police. She carried a switchblade and once had a tooth chipped when she was hit in the face with a bottle.[30]

It was the beating of a greaser friend by a Soc for no apparent reason that inspired Hinton to begin writing *The Outsiders* when she was fifteen and a sophomore in high school.[31] Filled with anger at the injustice of the situation, Hinton was expressing her fury when she began her novel by having her main character, Ponyboy Curtis, attacked and beaten by Socs as he makes his way home from the movies.

As she was writing *The Outsiders*, Hinton was searching for reality, something she felt was missing in "the inane junk lining the teenage shelf in the library."[32] She wanted to capture it all: the "drive-in social jungle, the behind the scenes politicking that goes on in big schools, the cruel social system in which if you can afford to snub every fourth person you meet, you are popular."[33] She

> **It was the beating of a greaser friend by a Soc for no apparent reason that inspired Hinton to begin writing *The Outsiders* when she was fifteen.**

began writing the kind of book she wanted to read, one that contained characters and concerns that she cared about. She was so in tune with the story she wanted to tell, that she did not even need to draw up an outline. All forty single-spaced pages of her first draft were written from her emotions.

Each time she wrote a revised draft, she added more details.

It took Hinton a year and a half to write *The Outsiders*. While she completed the novel, she was facing another life-changing event. Around the time she began to write the story, Hinton's father was diagnosed with a brain tumor. His health continued to decline, and while Lillian spent long hours with Grady Hinton in the hospital, Susie spent much of the time alone, writing at the dining room table. "The sicker he became, the harder she worked," said Lillian.[34] Hinton's father died when Hinton was a high school junior, just as she was completing the book. His sickness and death contributed to the emotional impact of *The Outsiders*. All of the real-life emotions that Hinton was facing over the prospect of losing her father were poured into her writing.

Hinton did not originally write *The Outsiders* for publication; however, at the urging of a friend's mother and another author, she sent her completed manuscript off to an agent. Hinton finished her senior year at Will Rogers High School uneventfully, but she left on graduation day bearing two things: a high school diploma and a contract from Viking Press offering her $1,000 to publish *The Outsiders*.[35]

Chapter 3

As Good as Gold

The Outsiders begins and ends with the same lines: "When I stepped out into the bright sunlight from the darkness of the movie house, I had only two things on my mind: Paul Newman and a ride home."[1]

The composition Ponyboy Curtis writes for his English class begins with these words. It is an account of the events that take place between two rival groups, the greasers and Socs, in Tulsa, Oklahoma, over the course of several days. Ponyboy and his two older brothers, Darry and Sodapop, are from a lower-class neighborhood. Because they live on the wrong side of town, they are called greasers by the rich kids. Their parents were killed in a car accident eight months before the story begins, and so the brothers are orphans who only have each other. Darry, a football player who gave up his future to take care of his brothers, serves as their father figure. Sodapop, the middle child, is a sensitive but happy-go-lucky high school dropout.

The gang rivalry that Ponyboy writes about in *The Outsiders* mirrors what was really happening at Will Rogers High School while Hinton was a student there. With their fancy clothes and expensive cars, the Socs were the in-crowd. Their parents' money and extravagant lifestyles set them apart from *The Outsiders*, the children of the working class.

Ponyboy begins his composition assignment by writing about how he is followed on the way home from the movies by members of the Socs in a red Corvair. Darry and Sodapop, along with two of their friends, Dallas Winston and the knife-wielding Two-Bit Matthews, rescue Ponyboy from the Socs. Later that night, Ponyboy, Dallas, and another greaser, Johnny Cade, sneak into the drive-in theatre to meet Cherry and Marcia, two Soc girls. The Socs learn of this and confront the greasers after the movie. To avoid another fight, Cherry leaves with Bob Sheldon, the leader of the Socs and the group's chief fighter.

Later, Ponyboy and Johnny reminisce about their lives as they stare at the stars while lying down in a vacant lot. Hinton uses this personal moment between the two to fill in some of their background information. Like Ponyboy, Johnny is living without the security and protection of

Ponyboy (C. Thomas Howell) and Johnny Cade (Ralph Macchio) in a scene from the 1983 film adaptation of *The Outsiders*.

his parent; his father physically abuses him and emotionally ignores him. Johnny is so neglected that the only people who care for him are the members of his greaser gang. The lack of parents is a bond Ponyboy and Johnny share, and both boys look to the fellow members of their greaser gang to be substitute family.

When Ponyboy gets home later that night, he is confronted by Darry, who, in his role of father figure to his younger brother, has been waiting up for him to come home. When Darry admonishes Ponyboy about the lateness of the hour, Ponyboy resents his brother's overprotectiveness and runs away to escape it. He takes Johnny with him, but the two only get as far as the park before meeting up once again with Bob Sheldon and the Socs. The tensions of the night erupt into a fight, and Johnny, in self-defense, kills Bob with a knife.

Running from the law, the boys hide out in a church in a nearby town for five days. They are visited occasionally by Dally (short for Dallas), who brings them food. Most of their time in hiding is spent reading *Gone With the Wind* and analyzing the poetry of Robert Frost. One Frost poem in particular, titled "Nothing Gold Can Stay," makes an impression on the two boys. The final lines of the poem ominously read, "So dawn goes down to day/ Nothing gold can stay."

Although he claims that he does not understand what the poem means, the fact that Ponyboy has memorized the poem is "another clue to his character's depth. This poem symbolizes the death of his parents, the goodness of life with them, and the inevitability that all of life will change."[2] Later, in a letter to Ponyboy, Johnny will offer a more optimistic view of the poem. His explanation of "staying gold" is that it means we should always remember the way things appeared to us in our youth. That we should try to view the world the way children do—with wonder and awe—and never lose sight of the endless possibilities life offers.

Eventually Johnny decides to turn himself in to the police for killing Bob, and after eating at a restaurant one night with Dally, the boys start out for home. On the way, they pass the church that had been Ponyboy and Johnny's hideaway. It is on fire and the boys wonder if it is burning because of their carelessness with cigarettes. There is a group of children inside, and Ponyboy and Johnny rush into the burning church in an attempt to save them. Johnny is seriously injured when a burning timber falls on his back, and he is taken to the hospital. Ponyboy and Dally are also injured, but the children are saved. Later that same night, the greasers and Socs have another confrontation, and this time the greasers win. Ponyboy rushes to the hospital to tell Johnny, only to find him close to

---

None of the events in the book are taken from life, but how the kids think and live and feel is for real.

---

death. With his last words, Johnny quotes from Robert Frost, telling Ponyboy to "stay gold."

The death of Johnny, whom he considered to be his best friend, causes Dallas to go berserk in a suicidal way: he robs a grocery store and is then shot and killed by the police when he raises an unloaded gun at them.

Ponyboy, who received a concussion in the fight with the Socs, must stay in bed for a few days. While recuperating, he experiences denial and confusion; he cannot accept Johnny's death, and he believes it was he, not Johnny, who killed Bob. He plans to confess to the murder at a hearing about Bob's death, but he is cleared of any wrongdoing before he is able to confess. Ponyboy feels dead inside until he receives one last symbolic message from Johnny: a letter tucked away inside his copy of *Gone With the Wind*. "Stay gold," Johnny had written to Ponyboy. These words are enough to bring Ponyboy around to an acceptance of the truth and a willingness to change his life. He begins his composition, thereby ending the novel with the very same lines that began it.[3]

Several themes set *The Outsiders* apart from the young adult literature that had come before it. Perhaps the most obvious difference is the violence. Knifings, beatings, threats, and other forms of aggression were written about in *The Outsiders* as never before. Teenagers living without parental authority, and the graphic accounts of how differences in social classes affect the young, were also new themes for young adult literature.

At the same time, there is a softer side to *The Outsiders*. Themes of hope, of possibility, and of the ability to change one's life are also played out in the plot of the story. This surprising contradiction has to do chiefly with the main character, Ponyboy Curtis. Despite the rough environment in which he lives and the harsh realities of his life, Ponyboy displays a gentler side of his character. Hinton uses Frost's poem, "Nothing Gold Can Stay" to show the poetic soul that hides underneath his self-styled greaser exterior. "Nothing Gold Can Stay" was selected for *The Outsiders* because Hinton had read it in her creative writing class, enjoyed it, and thought it appropriate for the book. She liked the enthusiasm the poem symbolized.[4] Like the overriding theme of *The Outsiders*, to Hinton "Nothing Gold Can Stay" represented the innocence that is lost as one grows older. "You lose your emotional commitments and I think that's what Frost had in mind. That's what I had in mind, even though I probably could not have articulated it at that time," said Hinton in 1979.[5]

Readers often wonder, how much of the plot of *The Outsiders* is based on real events? How many of the characters' personalities are based on real people? Hinton claims that the situations she wrote about in *The Outsiders* were actually a composite of things that happened to others. She says that none of the events in the book are taken from life, but how the kids think and live and feel is for real.[6] Although it appears that the greasers win in *The Outsiders*, Hinton tried not to be too hard on the Socs, because she had friends from both groups.[7]

The Outsiders eventually opened up a new genre of young adult literature called "The New Realism."

One of the reasons *The Outsiders* is such a profound novel has to do with its characterization, especially of the protagonist, Ponyboy. One reviewer observed that while Ponyboy is a greaser from a lower-class background, Hinton convincingly developed his toughness, his warm and forgiving nature, and his moments of irrationality so that they could easily be associated with a teenager from any social background.[8] Hinton feels especially close to the character of Ponyboy and says that a lot of his thoughts are her thoughts,[9] and that he is probably the closest she has ever come to putting herself into a character.[10]

Most reviewers were quick to grasp *The Outsiders'* chief theme of the inequality of social classes and its impact on young people. Lillian Gerhardt, writing in *School Library Journal,* said that "Ponyboy . . . tells how it looks and feels from the wrong side of the tracks." She found *The Outsiders* to be a favorite book of young adults because it made them think about class and different life styles, while at the same time allowing them to question both. Gerhardt further praised Hinton as a writer who was "seeing and saying more with greater storytelling ability than many an older hand."[11] Nat Hentoff, writing in *The Atlantic Monthly*, applauded Hinton, the messenger, while finding fault with the message of *The Outsiders*. He claimed the novel's plot was sometimes "factitious," but that Hinton, "with an astute ear and a lively sense of the restless rhythms of the young, also explores the tenacious loyalties on both sides of the class divide." Hentoff felt *The Outsiders* had such a large following among young adult readers because "it stimulates their own feelings and questionings about class and differing life-styles."[12]

Reviewers were also aware that young people were so starved for realistic fiction that the literary merit of *The Outsiders* would not matter to them, as long as they could relate to the characters. One reviewer foretold that Ponyboy Curtis would be elevated to the status of folk hero.[13]

The Outsiders eventually opened up a new genre of young adult literature called "The New Realism." Some scholars of children's literature actually pinpoint the beginning of "this new genre" to the book's publication. *The Outsiders* brought gangs, violence, alcoholism, drug addiction, and class warfare to young adult literature.[14] Hinton used these ugly, yet realistic, scenarios to deliver her ultimate message: hope abounds.

> ## "The book comes to life through its characters and situation, their almost painful yearnings and loyalties, their honesty."
>
> ### —Jay Daly

"Serious" books for young readers began focusing on "the big D's": the concepts of death, divorce, disease, and drugs.[15] *The Outsiders* showed young adult readers that there is the ability to see things as they ideally should be, and not as they really are. When looked at from this point of view, one could say that *The Outsiders* is concerned mostly with idealism and not realism.[16]

Jay Daly, in his critical overview, *Presenting*

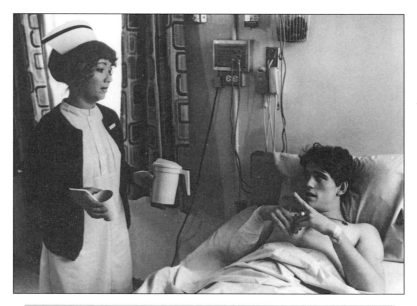

S.E. Hinton plays a cameo role as a nurse in this scene with Matt Dillon (as Dallas) in *The Outsiders* movie.

S.E. Hinton, wrote this about the impact of idealism and realism in *The Outsiders*:

> On its surface at least, *The Outsiders* is indeed a novel about the friction between social classes, in this case between the greasers and the Socs. It is also about the hunger for status, for a place in the pecking order, both inside and outside these groups. And it is about the violence that is so much a part of that particular place and time of life. These concerns are not, however, what make the book come alive. The book comes to life through its characters and situation, their almost painful yearnings and loyalties, their honesty. While parents and censors argued about violence and sensationalism, the readers responded to the characters, the people.[17]

Hinton would agree with Daly, for she sees as one of her strengths as a writer the ability to get to know her characters intimately. She always develops the personalities of her characters prior to developing a plot. As she writes, Hinton takes on her character's personality and she actually becomes the narrator.[18] About being a character writer, Hinton says:

> I always know my characters, exactly what they look like, their birthdays, what they like for breakfast. It doesn't matter if these things don't appear in the book. I still have to know. My characters are fictional. I get ideas from real people, sometimes, but my characters always exist only in my head . . . Those characters are as real to me as anyone else in my life, so much so that if I ran into one of them at the laundry I wouldn't be all that surprised.[19]

In all of her novels, Hinton's characters grow in some way, so that they are different at the end of the book from what they were when the book began.[20]

As well-developed as the characters of *The Outsiders* are, in the eyes of some reviewers, teachers, and librarians, characterization often was not enough to offset the violent nature of the book's plot. In her own defense, Hinton pointed out that the very same adults who objected to children reading about violence in *The Outsiders* had no problem with the subject matter when they allowed their children to watch violent and offensive television shows.[21] Only when violence is for a sensational effect should it be objected to in books for teenagers, wrote Hinton in the *New York Times Book Review*.[22]

Hinton addressed the issue of the violence in *The Outsiders* again in an interview with CBS Radio talk show host Don Swaim in 1987. Hinton said: "I've had so many kids write me and say: 'I realize from reading this book how stupid violence is.' I've never had a kid write me and say 'I got all hopped up and went out and beat up somebody after reading your book.'"[23]

Still, some adults proposed that the story line might encourage teens to idolize a life of lawlessness and destruction. Others felt it was wrong for young people to be exposed to violence in literature under any circumstances.[24] Forty years after it was first published, *The Outsiders* continues to cause controversy. The American Library Association listed it as number 41 in the "100 Most Frequently Challenged Books from

A scene from the 1990 television series adaptation of *The Outsiders*, featuring (from left to right) Boyd Kestner, David Arquette, Jay R. Ferguson, Rodney Harvey, Robert Rusler, and Harold Pruett.

1990–2000."[25] According to the American Booksellers Foundation, *The Outsiders* was number-three among the American Booksellers' most-banned and challenged books between 2004 and 2005.[26]

The Outsiders is not only about violence; themes of friendship, loyalty, and the futility of violence also are portrayed against the backdrop

> ## "I always know my characters, exactly what they look like, their birthdays, what they like for breakfast."
>
> **—S.E. Hinton**

of an unfriendly society. Although *The Outsiders* is a character-driven novel, Hinton makes use of plot to illustrate that although the Socs and greasers are enemies, the members of both groups feel the same way about important issues. This is a book with a message that rises above the violence, the gang mentality, and the abusive parents: No one has to be an outsider.[27]

Another interesting aspect of the violence issue had to do with the fact that sordid and gritty scenes portrayed in *The Outsiders* had been written by a girl. Most reviewers, as well as readers, assumed that the genderless "S.E." were the initials of a man. The book was made available to reviewers before the publication date, and information about Hinton had been released by the publisher. Gerhardt wrote: "Compassion was certainly evident throughout, but women have no corner on this quality," after learning that Hinton was female.[28] And, from the young, male adolescent point of view in *The Outsiders*, and the rough subject matter she addressed, it was easy to imagine that Hinton was tough and rough herself. Zena Sutherland, writing in *Saturday Review*, was one such reviewer under the impression that S.E. Hinton was as abrasive as her characters. "Having learned that S.E. Hinton is a girl, I looked forward with curiosity to meeting her. Prepared for a tough, shrewd, and possibly belligerent young woman, I met a pretty, gentle, and slightly nervous girl."[29]

In addition to her gender, Hinton's age baffled readers. She was nicknamed "the teenage wonder" because she had written the book when she was so young. It is generally thought that Hinton was able to write so convincingly about young adults because she was one herself. Sutherland called Hinton's writing style distinctive. She called Hinton "a teen-ager who is sensitive, honest and observant."[30]

Hinton's popularity with her intended readership—teens and young adults—has never been disputed. What has been questioned, however, is whether the popularity has been earned by her skill as a writer, or whether it is because she was in the right place, with the right story, at the right time.[31]

In spite of its controversial subject matter, in 1967 *The Outsiders* was chosen as one of the *New York Herald Tribune*'s Best Teenage Books and named a *Chicago Tribune* Book World Spring Book Festival Honor Book. In 1975, it received a Media and Methods Maxi Award and was named one of the Best Young Adult Books by the American Library Association. In 1979, *The Outsiders* received the Massachusetts Children's Book Award.

In the early 1980s, a group of high school students wrote to the Oscar-winning motion picture director, producer, and writer Francis Ford Coppola and asked him to make *The Outsiders* into a movie. Coppola obtained the rights from Hinton, who worked with him adapting the book to the screen. Hinton had a minor part in the movie playing a nurse. During the filming of the movie, most of the cast and crew referred to Hinton as "Mom."

In 1990, a television show based on *The Outsiders* was adapted by Fox television; it ran for fourteen weeks. In 2005, the movie version of *The Outsiders* debuted on DVD. It was also re-released for a limited run in theaters.

Chapter 4

"Growth Is Betrayal"

The Outsiders was the first of five novels written by Hinton about adolescent males trying to survive in violent and hostile environments. Writing *The Outsiders* had come relatively easy to Hinton; with no outlined plot, she had just sat down and written it, day after day, page after page, draft after draft. Not really knowing anything about the formal writing process, Hinton kept writing and rewriting until she was happy with the story.[1]

Hinton's second book, *That Was Then, This Is Now*, did not come to her so easily. By then Hinton was at the University of Tulsa, studying for a degree in education. A lot had changed in Hinton's life since she wrote *The Outsiders* in high school. For one thing, she was recognized as an author who had written a book that had shaken up the publishing world. With this accomplishment came demands on her time, such as fan letters to answer, interviews to give, and presentations to make.

The shy young author, who enjoyed spending time alone reading, writing, and horseback riding, suddenly found herself thrust into the limelight. It was a situation entirely unfamiliar to her. It was also unusual for the publishing industry to have a successful author who was so young. At times Hinton did not know how to handle the changes being an author brought into her life. She told an interviewer for *Seventeen*:

> The publisher thought that my being a teen-age writer was a good gimmick, and my close friends thought it was neat. But people I didn't know too well started treating me as though I were stuck-up. I had always been a smart-aleck kid, but after the book was published I knew I had to change or else people would think success was going to my head. So I became quiet—but people saw that as being stuck-up, too.[2]

Hinton, a "Teen-age Wonder" and "The Voice of the Youth," had found the niche in young adult publishing that had been waiting to be filled. Having seen what she could produce, young adult readers clamored for more realistic fiction from her. Hinton, however, had a problem: she could not write. Whether it was the success of *The Outsiders*, the demands on her time as an author, or the rigors of her college courses, Hinton found herself in the throes of something dreaded by every author: the inability to write, the sensation of feeling "stuck" known as writer's block.

Hinton's writer's block lasted for four years, and it was so severe that at times she could not even type a letter on the typewriter.[3] Writing only to please herself, as she had done with *The Outsiders*, had been fun, but writing as a profession, for an audience that expected only good stories, scared her.[4] After the success of *The Outsiders*, only a masterpiece would do.[5] Hinton became self-critical and constantly questioned her own ability as a writer. She wondered if *The Outsiders* had been merely a fluke. When it came

---

At times Hinton did not know how to handle the changes being an author brought into her life.

---

to writing, did she really know what she was doing? Soon she was facing not only writer's block, but depression as well.

In addition to not being able to write, Hinton was also depressed because she was starting to realize that she had selected the wrong college major. The money she was making from *The Outsiders* was paying for her college education. Because she liked being around children, Hinton had chosen to major in education and hoped to become a teacher. However, her student teaching had shown her that she did not have the nerve or physical stamina to teach. She found it hard not to become emotionally involved with her students.

At the end of the school day she could not leave her students and their problems behind, and she would spend her evenings at home worrying about them.[6] It was difficult to write when her mind was full of thoughts of her students.

There was another thing that was disturbing Hinton and contributing to her writer's block. As a college student, she had to do a lot of required reading for her courses. The reading exposed her to many fine pieces of literature. When Hinton compared *The Outsiders* to the writing of others, she found herself lacking. Rereading *The Outsiders* again at the age of twenty, she found it to be "the worse piece of trash I'd ever seen, and I magnified all its faults."[7]

Soon after enrolling at the University of Tulsa, Hinton met another student named David Inhofe in freshman biology class. The two began dating.

> **The message that Hinton wanted to convey . . . is one of "growth is betrayal."**

David was quick to recognize the gifted writer behind the depressed college student, and he encouraged Hinton to start writing another novel. To motivate her, he gave her a writing quota of two pages a day. If she met her quota, he rewarded her by taking her out that evening. If she did not write two pages, they did not go out.

The slow and laborious process of writing two pages a day continued for months. For her second book, Hinton's writing was more careful and controlled. She wanted each sentence to be perfect. When she had accumulated a stack of papers that looked like it contained enough material for a book, she sent it off to her publisher. The result was her second novel for young adults: *That Was Then, This Is Now*. It was written in 1970 and published in 1971.

There are many similarities between *That Was Then, This Is Now* and *The Outsiders*. Hinton's second book was also about a young man trying to make sense of his life. Both books are narrated in the first person from the main character's point of view. This technique, used in most of Hinton's books, allows the reader to instantly become involved with the protagonist. *That Was Then, This Is Now* is also similar to *The Outsiders* in that Hinton places the characters of both books in situations where they must learn to deal with life's problems without the help or guidance of caring adults. Both books contain graphic situations and scenes, and in both books it is Hinton's strong characters that carry the plot.

Hinton wanted to be sure her readers understood that *That Was Then, This Is Now* was not a sequel to *The Outsiders*. In *The Outsiders*, Hinton's main characters are positioned against society and the rules and regulations that govern its class system. In *That Was Then, This Is Now*, the conflict concerns the relationship between Bryon, who is sixteen years old, and his closest friend and unofficially adopted brother, Mark Jennings.

The cast of the 1985 film adaptation of *That Was Then, This Is Now* (clockwise, from top left): Jill Schoelen, Emilio Estevez, Craig Sheffer, Kim Delaney, Larry B. Scott, and Frank Howard.

Parents are absent in this book as well. Mark has lived with Bryon and his mother since he witnessed his own parents kill each other during an argument over Mark's parentage. Bryon's mother is in and out of the hospital, so the boys are mostly on their own.

Bryon and Mark have very different personalities. Bryon is involved in school and girls while Mark, who never really learned how to read well, becomes involved in drugs and crime. *That Was Then, This Is Now* takes place about a year after the events of *The Outsiders*. Ponyboy Curtis has a small role in Hinton's second novel when Bryon and his girlfriend, Cathy, meet him at a dance. Ponyboy's appearance connects the time and place of *The Outsiders* with *That Was Then, This Is Now*. There is still gang violence intertwined with Mark and Bryon's story. However, gang rivalry does not contribute as much to the setting of Hinton's second book as it does in the first. Still, Hinton remains true to the time of the novel, with its emphasis on hippies and drugs, especially LSD. When Bryon discovers that Mark has been dealing drugs, he turns him in to the police. Mark is sentenced to five years in the state reformatory, leaving Bryon to wish he was a kid again when he had all the answers. This explains the significance of the book's title: that was then, and this is now.[8]

The message that Hinton wanted to convey when she began writing *That Was Then, This Is Now* is one of "growth is betrayal." When she had completed the book she felt that she had been successful in getting the message out to her readers.[9] It is his betrayal of Mark that leads to Bryon's personal growth. And while, like *The Outsiders*, *That Was Then, This Is Now* had disturbing and ugly scenes, the book was said to have found a place in the understanding of today's young people's cultural problems.[10]

Hinton felt that her orderly, two-pages-a-day method for writing *That Was Then, This Is Now*

"[*That Was Then, This Is Now* is a] mature, disciplined novel, which excites a response in the reader and will be hard to forget."

—Michael Cart

---

made her second book much better than her first.[11] Michael Cart, writing in the *New York Times Book Review*, agreed. "Miss Hinton uses the phrase 'if only' to underline her theme that growth can be dangerous," he wrote, and he called *That Was Then, This Is Now* a "mature, disciplined novel, which excites a response in the reader and will be hard to forget."[12]

The publication of *That Was Then, This Is Now* was personally significant to Hinton. It proved that her success with *The Outsiders* was more than a coincidence or a fluke. She was an author who could write more than one book. *That Was Then, This Is Now* demonstrated that she was expanding her themes and writing techniques, and it showed promise that they would continue to improve in future books.[13]

In 1971, the year it was published, *That Was Then, This Is Now* received an American Library Association Best Books for Young Adults award. It also was chosen as a *Chicago Tribune* Book World Spring Book Festival Honor Book the same year. In 1978, it received a Massachusetts Children's Book Award, and in 1985 a movie version of *That Was Then, This Is Now* was released by Paramount Pictures.

Hinton graduated from the University of Tulsa in 1970, and later that year, she and David Inhofe were married. They traveled in Europe for six months after their wedding and then settled in Palo Alto, California, while David attended graduate school. In 1973 they moved back to Tulsa and have lived in and around Tulsa ever since.

Chapter 5

Brotherly Love

Four years passed before another S.E. Hinton novel appeared in the bookstores. In 1975, when Hinton was about twenty-five years old, *Rumble Fish* was published. Once again, and almost without introduction, Hinton dove into a gritty story told from a young adolescent male's point of view. As in her two previous books, the strong theme of brotherhood runs through *Rumble Fish*.

The story of *Rumble Fish* begins with these words: "I was hanging out at Benny's, playing pool, when I heard Biff Wilcox was looking to kill me."[1] The narrator is Rusty-James, a teenager with more street smarts than intelligence, who is trying to make a name for himself as a tough boy. Rusty-James narrates the story to his friend Steve in a series of flashbacks to events that occurred five years earlier. He tells how he admires his older brother, the Motorcycle Boy, a greaser hero, and wants to be just like him. Rusty-James relies on the Motorcycle Boy to save him when he gets into situations he is unable to handle. The boys' mother deserted them and moved to California, and their father drinks and is irresponsible; when Rusty-James was two years old, his father left him alone in the house for three days. Now the brothers, in typical Hinton style, are left to watch out for, and take care of, each other.[2]

Hinton first thought Steve should tell the story, and she wrote one entire version of the book with Steve as the narrator. However, Steve was too articulate, and he could tell the story too easily. Rusty-James is not good at expressing his feelings or talking about things that matter. Telling the story through a character like Rusty-James who is not good at expressing himself made the book more challenging for Hinton to write.[3]

Hinton had been reading about color symbolism and mythology around the time she was writing *Rumble Fish*, so this book contains more symbolism than do Hinton's earlier books.[4] For example, Hinton did not give the Motorcycle Boy a proper name because she wanted to emphasize how he is alienated from everyone and everything. The Motorcycle Boy cannot identify with anything, he cannot find anything that he wants to do or be.[5] Although he is older than Rusty-James, the latter demonstrates greater maturity.

Like many young people around his age, the

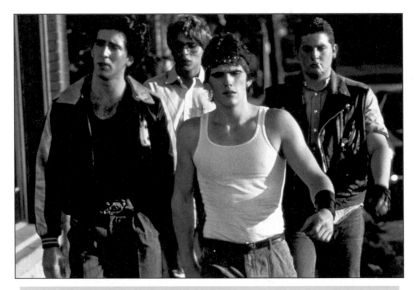

Some of the cast in a scene from the 1983 film adaptation of *Rumble Fish* (from left to right): Nicolas Cage, Vincent Spano, Matt Dillon, and Christopher Penn.

Motorcycle Boy is searching for meaning in his life. Hinton made this character color-blind because he is unable to compromise. He interprets life in black and white, and he usually walks away from a situation rather than sticking around and resolving it. This is what ultimately kills him.[6] The Motorcycle Boy dies in *Rumble Fish* in a way similar to Dallas in *The Outsiders*: he is gunned down after breaking into a pet store and setting the animals free.[7] The Motorcycle Boy had taken a special interest in the rumble fish, the Siamese fighting fish which must be kept in separate containers to keep them from killing one another. He wonders if the rumble fish will fight to the death if they are set free in the river, but he does not live to find out.

Hinton was inspired to write *Rumble Fish* and, in particular, the character of the Motorcycle Boy from a picture of a boy on a motorcycle that had appeared in *Saturday Review* in 1967. Hinton still has the framed picture. She just felt she had to write about him, and she first did so in a short story she wrote for the 1968 edition of *Nimrod*, the literary supplement to University of Tulsa Alumni Magazine. Hinton was a junior in college at the time. Caught in the throes of writer's block, the short story was the only piece of fiction she wrote between *The Outsiders* and *That Was Then, This Is Now*.[8]

Rusty-James shares similarities with Hinton's earlier characters. Like Ponyboy Curtis in *The Outsiders* and Bryon in *That Was Then, This Is*

Now, Rusty-James's life is changed forever by the incidents that take place in the course of the story. In his quest to grow up, Rusty-James loses his brother, his reputation, and his girlfriend, Patty.[9] Although the Motorcycle Boy is killed in the story, it is Rusty-James that readers of *Rumble Fish* identify with most. However, his personality is not as strong as Ponyboy's or Bryon's, and because of this some of Hinton's readers felt let down. They expected Rusty-James to have the same strong personality as Hinton's previous two characters.

At the end of the book, Rusty-James goes deaf and color-blind. Hinton wrote this so that a parallel would exist between the two brothers. She wanted to show two completely different people: one very complex (the Motorcycle Boy) and one simple (Rusty-James) who went through the same battering set of circumstances and came out relatively the same at the end (color-blind).[10]

> **"[*Rumble Fish*] packed a punch that will leave readers of any age reeling."**
>
> **—Jane Abramson**

Rumble Fish is the shortest of Hinton's young adult novels. Although she found it difficult to write from the point of view of someone like Rusty-James, who is not articulate, observant, or intelligent, she was very happy with the way the book turned out.[11] She found Rusty-James to be her biggest challenge as a writer.[12]

With the publication of *Rumble Fish*, Hinton was accumulating a body of work and giving reviewers the opportunity to compare the main characters and plots of all her stories. Overall, the narrative and dialogue were notable in Hinton's third book. Reviewers were eager to position *Rumble Fish* against *The Outsiders* and *That Was Then, This Is Now*, and in doing so gave *Rumble Fish* mixed reviews. Margery Fisher, writing in the British journal *Growing Point*, said: ". . . of the three striking books by this young author, *Rumble Fish* seems the most carefully structured and the most probing."[13] *Publishers Weekly* declared "Hinton a brilliant novelist."[14] Jane Abramson wrote in *School Library Journal* that "it is Rusty-James, emotionally burnt out at 14, who is the ultimate victim," and that *Rumble Fish* "packed a punch that will leave readers of any age reeling."[15]

Not all reviewers, however, liked *Rumble Fish*. Anita Silvey, writing in *Horn Book*, remarked that "[Hinton] is no longer a teenager writing about teenagers today." Silvey also said that *Rumble Fish* raises the question whether, as an adult, Hinton will ever have much of importance to say to young readers. Silvey thought the book was "unsatisfying" and proof that Hinton's further writing potential was "unpromising."[16] Another reviewer said *Rumble Fish* had bleak points and that the Motorcycle Boy "clanks through the story like a symbol never quite made flesh."[17]

One of the most positive views came from Jay Daly, who wrote in his book, *Presenting S.E. Hinton*:

Mickey Rourke as the Motorcycle Boy in a scene from *Rumble Fish*.

"In the end we respond to *Rumble Fish* in a much deeper way than we do to *That Was Then, This Is Now*." While commenting on what he called the too-obvious symbolism found in *Rumble Fish*, he said that overall he felt it provoked an emotional response as opposed to the earlier book, which he felt provoked an intellectual reaction. The book "works as a novel . . . [t]here is a name usually given to this kind of success. It is called art," he wrote.[18]

Rumble Fish was given an American Library Association Best Book for Young Adult Award in 1975. The same year, *School Library Journal* named *Rumble Fish* one of the Best Books of the Year. In 1982, the New Mexico Library

---

"[T]here is a name usually given to this kind of success. It is called art."

—Jay Daly

Association gave *Rumble Fish* a "Land of Enchantment" book award.

In 1983, *Rumble Fish* was made into a movie by Francis Ford Coppola, the same director who produced the movie version of *The Outsiders*. Hinton cowrote the screenplay with Coppola. She also worked as an adviser on the movie and had a small part playing a prostitute. Coppola shot the film in black and white to emphasize the Motorcycle Boy's colorblindness.

Hinton, who has never been one to join a group, found working on the set with actors and producers an exciting experience. Those working on the movie accepted her instantly, and it was the first time she had felt at home in a group situation.[19]

It was also a good experience for Francis Ford Coppola. He said: "When I met Susie, it was confirmed to me that she was not just a younger people's novelist, but a real American novelist. For me, the primary thing about her books is that the characters come across as very real. Her dialogue is memorable, and her prose is striking. Often a paragraph of her descriptive prose sums up something essential and stays with you."[20]

Hinton was happy with the movie version of *Rumble Fish*. As for *Rumble Fish* the book, Hinton has said it is the book she is proudest of in a literary way—she felt it was the easiest to read, the hardest to understand, and definitely the hardest to write.[21]

By the time *Rumble Fish* was published, readers were quite used to Hinton's formula of tough male youths narrating in first-person a story about the fight to find meaningful lives in a violent world devoid of grown-ups.[22] Therefore, they were not surprised when Hinton's next book, *Tex*, was written in much the same format.

Tex McCormick is Hinton's favorite character. Out of all her characters, she says he is the one who is the least tough, but the strongest.[23] Tex is fourteen years old, and his older brother, seventeen-year-old

Mason, looks after him in their run-down house. The boys do not get along well, and, among other things, Mason thinks Tex is simple-minded. Their mother died of pneumonia and their father travels with a rodeo. He has been away from the boys for five months and has not sent them money in a while.

Tex looks to his horse, Negrito, for companionship, while Mason, a worldlier senior in high school, hopes to get to college on a basketball scholarship. When Mason has to sell some of the family's horses, including Negrito, to pay the bills, the relationship between the boys further deteriorates. Tex is having difficulty in school as well as at home, and he believes running away to find Negrito will solve all his problems. However, Mason goes after Tex and brings him home.

Eventually, the two brothers are kidnapped by a character from one of Hinton's previous novels—Mark from *That Was Then, This Is Now*—who was sentenced to five years in jail for dealing drugs and has escaped. Mark is hitchhiking and Tex, who is driving a pick-up truck, stops to give him a ride. Mark holds a gun on Mason, but Tex cleverly drives the truck into a ditch, and Mark is killed by the police.

Tex and Mason's father, who is in

> "[*Tex*] is about . . . love, which can't cure anything but sometimes makes the unbearable bearable."
>
> —S.E. Hinton

Dallas, Texas, sees a news report of the kidnapping on television and decides to return home. Tex then learns from Mason that the man he thought of as his father really is not. Shaken and in emotional shock, Tex accompanies a friend on a drug deal and ends up in the hospital with a bullet wound. Eventually Mason and Tex reconcile. By the end of the story, Tex tells Mason he will take care of himself by getting a job working with horses, and he convinces Mason to go to college.[24]

Hinton explained in publicity material produced by Delacorte Press that *Tex* is about "relationships, which are complicated for simple people . . . love, which can't cure anything but sometimes makes the unbearable bearable; and being a teen-ager, which is problem enough for anybody."[25]

Hinton did not feel that Tex was like her on a personal level, but he was the narrator that she most enjoyed being.[26] He is Hinton's most childlike character, but also the one who makes the most progress growing up. In short, Hinton called Tex her favorite child.[27] She describes Tex as "capable of thinking, [but] he has to be made to think; he relies on instinct instead of intellect. And basically his instincts are good." He is "capable of violence, but not malice; he has to learn things the hard way—a basically happy person trying to deal with unhappiness. I envied his total lack of suspicion," said Hinton.[28]

Hinton's character development in *Tex* was but one of her writing techniques that reviewers liked.

S.E. Hinton and Matt Dillon on the set of *Tex*.

Marilyn Kaye, in *School Library Journal*, commented that Hinton's style had matured since she exploded onto the young adult scene in 1967. She wrote: "Hinton's raw energy has not been tamed—it's been cultivated."[29] Jay Daly called *Tex* an example of mature, polished storytelling, "Hinton's most successful effort."[30] Margery Fisher, a reviewer for England's *Growing Point*, praised Hinton by saying she "has achieved that illusion of reality which any fiction writer aspires to and which few ever completely achieve."[31]

Some reviewers thought *Tex* was too plot-heavy. *New York Times Book Review* contributor Paxton Davis believes there is too much going on in *Tex* and that the number of unusual events occurring in the story strains credulity. He wrote that even by the standards of today's fiction, S.E. Hinton's vision of contemporary teenage life is riper than warrants belief.[32] Another reviewer, Lance Salway, writing in *Signal* said that "*Tex* is theatrical, but a writer as good as Hinton can carry it off effortlessly; one believes implicitly in the characters and cares what happens to them."[33]

In 1979, *Tex* received the American Library Association Best Books for Young Adults Award, and it was named a *School Library Journal* Best Book of the Year. In 1980, the book received a New York Public Library "Book for the Teen-Age" citation, and in 1981 *Tex* was nominated to receive an American Book Award.

Tex, the first of Hinton's novels to be made into a motion picture, was released in 1982 by Disney

Studios. Matt Dillon, an up-and-coming star, played the lead role of Tex. Dillon had read Hinton's books and had especially enjoyed *Rumble Fish*. However, he had not realized S.E. Hinton is a woman. "From reading your books, Susie, I thought you were a man," Dillon said to Hinton the first time he met her.[34]

Tex was filmed in Tulsa, and Hinton served as an adviser to the production and was involved with directing, scriptwriting, and casting. Hinton's own horse, Toyota, portrayed Negrito, and Hinton coached Dillon on how to ride a horse. Dillon ended up acting in three of the four Hinton novels that were adapted for the movies. He and Hinton have developed a friendship over the years.

Hinton had thought long and hard about allowing Disney Studios to make *Tex* into a movie. She was afraid that the story would be "sugar coated" and that the scenes involving sex, drugs, and violence would be removed to make the movie acceptable for younger viewers. In the end, Hinton was pleased with the way the movie version of *Tex* turned out. "There's one other nice thing about the movies," she said. "There's always somebody else to blame. With a novel, you have to take all the blame yourself.[35]

Chapter 6

Taming the Star Runner

Almost nine years passed before Hinton produced another book. Much of this time was spent working on the four movies that had been created from her novels. Also, in 1983, her son, Nicholas David Inhofe was born, adding a whole new dimension to her life.

In 1988, Hinton became the first recipient of the Young Adult Services Division of *School Library Journal* Author Achievement Award, also known as the Margaret A. Edwards Award. This award was given to Hinton for her career achievement in young adult literature.[1] The award honors authors whose "book or books, over a period of time, have been accepted by young people as an authentic voice that continues to illuminate their experiences and emotions, giving insight into their lives.[2]

Later that same year Hinton released *Taming the Star Runner*, the story of fifteen-year-old Travis Harris. Travis almost kills his abusive stepfather with a fireplace poker, and he is sent off to his Uncle Ken's Oklahoma horse ranch instead of juvenile prison. Travis's uncle is not without his own problems; he is going through a divorce, and having young Travis living with him on the ranch takes some getting used to. Travis is having a difficult

---

Hinton sees writing from a boy's point of view as a way of reaching an entire audience of young readers—both male and female.

---

time himself; he cannot make friends with the rural students, whom he calls hick jocks and hick nerds. To get away from his uncle, Travis spends time at the barn, watching Casey Kincaid, who runs a riding school at the ranch, train her stallion, Star Runner. Casey is three years older than Travis and he admires her bravery in trying to tame the wild, edgy horse. Eventually Travis and Casey fall in love.

One thing that helps Travis cope with his fragmented life is writing. He has written a book which his stepfather will not allow him to publish because he does not like the way Travis has portrayed him. Travis's mother, however, sides with Travis and gives her consent for the book to be published. Just when it looks like life is beginning to settle down, a tornado tears through the ranch. Star Runner is killed, presumably after being struck by lightning. As the book ends, Travis and his uncle are forced to move off the ranch.[3]

Taming the Star Runner was the first of Hinton's books to be written in the third-person. Her loyal readers wondered about this switch in writing style, and they speculated that Hinton might be losing her touch for writing for young adults. Making herself the narrator, as she had with Ponyboy, Bryon, Rusty-James, and Tex, had placed Hinton inside the story. Telling a story in the first-person also made it easier for her readers to identify with the protagonist.

Hinton's son, Nick, is the main reason Hinton wrote *Taming the Star Runner* in the third-person. Nick was four years old when Hinton was writing the book, and she was so emotionally involved with him that she was incapable of writing in the first-person and becoming a completely new character.[4]

Although *Taming the Star Runner* is not told in the first-person, it is still told from a young male's point of view. Hinton has often been criticized and called sexist for ignoring the female point of view in her books. Hinton has tried, but she cannot write from a female point of view because she identifies with the male point of view too strongly. She feels her alter ego is clearly a fifteen-year-old boy.[5] When she first began writing as a teenager, she believed she had a male mind. Now she thinks she has a female mind that did not conform to the female culture at the time.[6] It has long been known in the publishing field that girls will read books written for boys, but boys seldom read books written for girls.[7] Therefore, Hinton sees writing from a boy's point of view as a way of reaching an entire audience of young readers—both male and female.

Hinton calls *Taming the Star Runner* "a horse story, a love story, and a story of the different forms art can take."[8] Readers will notice certain similarities between Travis's story and Hinton's. Both are horse-lovers. Also, like Hinton, Travis has a book accepted by a New York publisher while he is a teenager.

As was typical of Hinton's other books, reviewers either loved or hated *Taming the Star Runner*. Charlene Strickland wrote in *School Library Journal* that the book's plot is sparse and built around a predominately bleak theme. She also felt that tough guy Travis will appeal to a certain readership, however, others will find him forgettable, especially compared to his fictional predecessors [Ponyboy, Bryon, Rusty-James, and Tex].[9]

> **"No one can speak to the adolescent psyche the way S.E. Hinton can."**
>
> **—Nancy Vasilakis**

Nancy Vasilakis wrote in *Horn Book* that Hinton had not lost her touch with this, her fifth novel. "It has been generally agreed that no one can speak to the adolescent psyche the way S.E. Hinton can," she said.[10] Patty Campbell wrote in the *New York Times Book Review* that "Travis was just another tough young Galahad in black T-shirt and leather jacket. . . . [Hinton's] genius lies in that she has been able to give each of her five protagonists . . . a unique voice and a unique story. S.E. Hinton continues to grow in strength as a young adult novelist."[11]

Other reviewers agreed. One felt *Taming the Star Runner* was "Hinton's most mature and accomplished work"[12] and that "Hinton continues to grow more reflective in her books, but her great understanding not of what teen-agers are but of what they can hope to be, is undiminished."[13]

In 1989, the American Library Association (ALA) presented *Taming the Star Runner* with two awards. It was selected to be a "Best Book for Young Adults" and a Quick Pick for reluctant young adult readers.

After writing *Taming the Star Runner*, Hinton took a seven-year break from writing books. During this time she wrote screenplays, television scripts, and advertisements, but mainly she was a mother to young Nick. She was so emotionally committed to being a mother that there was no story within her to tell.[14]

Chapter 7

Kids and Puppies

Although the protagonists of Hinton's first five books were all young males grappling with personal anxieties of one sort or another, Hinton had, as Patty Campbell indicated, given them their own voices. The overall themes of their stories—loyalty, betrayal, and finding oneself—may have been similar, but each voice was distinct from the others. Each narrator had his own story to tell and his own voice in which to tell it.[1]

As she aged into her thirties, Hinton continued to write for young adults because she understood young people and really liked them. She remembered what it was like to be a teenager and she knew many teens nobody listened to, paid attention to, or wanted around.[2] She kept writing about characters in their teens because she saw it as "an interesting time of life . . . [when] ideals are slamming up against the walls of compromise."[3]

In 1995, Hinton made a departure from her signature style of writing for young adults to write books for a completely different audience: elementary-school-age children. That year Hinton published two children's books that were both somewhat autobiographical in nature. She branched into shorter children's books because she was busy raising her son and she did not have the emotional energy to put into a novel. Although childrearing was demanding in and of itself, Hinton knew that when the time was right, she would get back to writing. "It's all I ever wanted to do. I began in grade school and it's all I know how to do," she said.[4]

Big David, Little David is Hinton's first picture book. It is based on a joke Hinton and her husband David played on their son, Nick. When he was in kindergarten, Nick met a boy who was a miniature version of his father. He even had the same name. "He's not you, is he?" Nick asks his father in the book, and Nick's parents convince him that little David and big David are one and the same. They keep up the joke until Parents' Night at School. Then for the first time big David and little David are in the same place at the same time, and Nick finally realizes they are not the same person.[5]

School Library Journal had a difficult time with Hinton's switch from a writer of young adult fiction to a writer of picture books. "The warm fuzzy family story definitely has charm and abounds with clever humor that's sure to tickle adults and may delight gifted children, but it's likely to baffle most kids," wrote one reviewer.[6] *Booklist* agreed, stating that "this offbeat picture book has a certain ambiguity that might make preschoolers uncomfortable. Slightly older children, though, will probably enjoy the story."[7]

Publishers Weekly, on the other hand, felt Hinton "shifts easily into picture-book gear in this genuinely funny look at the unorthodox dilemma facing a likable youngster named Nick . . . Hinton gives her tale an innovative twist as clever Nick manages to get the last laugh."[8]

Hinton commented that *Big David, Little David* is the closest book to her real life, and that it is almost true word for word.[9]

That same year Hinton released *The Puppy Sister*, a fantasy book written for elementary-school-age children. *The Puppy Sister* is about sibling rivalry between a boy and his dog, and it is the most autobiographical of all of Hinton's books.[10] Once again, Hinton's son, Nick, is a main character of the book. Like the real Nick, the Nick in *The Puppy Sister* is an only child who really wants a baby sister. In real life, Nick did not like animals and was even a little afraid of dogs, but when he was eight years old, Hinton got him an

> **"It's all I ever wanted to do."**
>
> —S.E. Hinton on writing.

Australian shepherd puppy named Aleasha. The sibling rivalry was so intense between the boy and dog that Nick once accused Hinton of loving the dog more than she loved him. "Honey . . . it's not true. I love you more: you're housebroken," Hinton told him.[11]

Hinton knew the story of puppy–boy rivalry was a good one, but she needed a hook. Nick provided it when the three of them came home from a walk one day and Nick asked his mother when Aleasha would turn into a person.[12]

Hinton tells the story in the first-person from Aleasha's point of view. It is the first book she has written from a non-male perspective. Aleasha does not want to stay a dog. She wants to become a human like Nick and eat at the table and go trick

> **Hinton was reaching the children and the grandchildren of those who had read her young adult novels in the 1960s and 1970s.**

or treating on Halloween. Gradually, Aleasha stands upright on two legs, sheds her dog fur, and starts to speak. All this is fine with Nick's mom and dad who, after getting over the shock that their dog is turning human, welcome Aleasha into the family as the daughter they never had. They keep the secret of Aleasha's transformation from the nosy neighbors, but have to tell a pediatrician friend when Aleasha gets sick. In the end, the explanation given for Aleasha is that the family has adopted a little girl.[13]

The Puppy Sister was written for children in the 7–11 year-old-age range. Hinton let Nick read *The Puppy Sister* while it was still in manuscript because he was so much a part of it.[14]

Susanna Rodell, writing in the *New York Times Book Review*, found the plot and characterization of *The Puppy Sister* to be implausible, but she stated that "children old enough to read but not yet gripped by adolescent cynicism will have a lot of fun with Nick and Aleasha."[15]

"[T]his irresistible fantasy can take its place alongside *Stuart Little* and *Babe the Gallant Pig*," wrote a reviewer in *Publishers Weekly*.[16] However, *School Library Journal* found *The Puppy Sister* contained "too little conflict and character development [which] result in a fantasy that falls flat."[17]

With the release of *Big David, Little David* and *The Puppy Sister*, Hinton was reaching the children and the grandchildren of those who had read her young adult novels in the 1960s and 1970s. In 1995, *The Puppy Sister* was awarded the Parents' Choice Silver Honor Book.

Chapter 8

Hawkes Harbor

Once Hinton's son went away to college, Hinton once again entered a stage in her life where she was free to devote herself to writing.[1] In 2004, Hinton's first adult novel, *Hawkes Harbor*, was published. It had been nine years since the release of her two children's books and sixteen years after the release of her last young adult novel, *Taming the Star Runner*.

Hawkes Harbor, a montage of high-seas adventure and vampire horror, tells the story of Jamie Sommers, an orphan raised by nuns in a Bronx, New York, orphanage. After meeting an unsavory Irishman named Kellen Quinn in Hawaii, the two take to the sea to search for danger and adventure. Their experiences include gunrunning, smuggling, foreign prisons, pirates, sharks, and murder. The entire time, Jamie is running from the past and avoiding the anger of his childhood.

The two end up in the fictional town of Hawkes Harbor in Delaware. Hawkes Harbor has many strange things about it, such as a high rate of insanity, the disappearance of residents, and an unusually strong cold current. Jamie meets Grenville Hawkes, after whom the town is named. Grenville is really a vampire, and Jamie becomes his servant. Jamie's association with Grenville is the undoing of both himself and Kell Quinn.[2]

Jamie ends up in a private psychiatric institution called Terrace View Asylum where he is treated by Dr. McDevitt. In the course of his treatment, he relates his sordid past to the psychiatrist. To do this, Hinton makes use of flashbacks to tell the story.

Telling the story in retrospect is a writing technique that worked well for Hinton in *The Outsiders*, as well as in some of her other young adult novels. In *Hawkes Harbor*, the flashbacks are not always in chronological order, and in one part of the story, Hinton has even included a flashforward.

Hinton spent five years researching and writing *Hawkes Harbor*, which was inspired by her reading of Robert Louis Stevenson's *Treasure Island* and Charles Dickens's *David Copperfield*.[3] Though *Hawkes Harbor* embraces themes quite different from those in Hinton's earlier books, it still has the hallmark of classic Hinton writing: the plot is driven by the characters and focuses on relationships.[4]

One difference between *Hawkes Harbor* and Hinton's earlier books is its setting. *Hawkes Harbor* takes place in a number of locations, from the Andaman Sea to the French Riviera to New Orleans. Hinton's young adult novels are set in one place. Hinton sees a larger setting as appropriate for an adult novel. "I'm out of high school. I'm all over the world instead of in one place," Hinton told an interviewer for the *Austin Chronicle*, shortly after *Hawkes Harbor* was published.[5]

> "A contemporary *Treasure Island* with a genre-bending twist."
>
> —*Publishers Weekly* on *Hawkes Harbor*

Hawkes Harbor came about because Hinton was getting "itchy" to write something different[6] and wanted to write an adventure story.[7] Hinton also took a different approach to writing *Hawkes Harbor*. She did not write it in chronological order. She just picked a scene that she wanted to write and wrote it.[8] Using this writing technique, Hinton actually wrote the last chapter first.

Hinton chose to set *Hawkes Harbor* in the 1960s because she did not want to "deal with technology."[9] It is a setting she is familiar with from her earlier books. Although *Hawkes Harbor* is written for adults, the book contains an "outsider" element. Jamie could very well be an older version of one of the characters of any of Hinton's young adult books.

Hawkes Harbor contains a little bit of everything: comedy, action, suspense, the supernatural, and fantasy. As with her children's books, acceptance of Hinton's writing in this new genre was hard to come by. Elizabeth Hand, writing in the *Washington Post*, called *Hawkes Harbor* "a shambles" and a "rambling, episodic mess. . . . It's sad, and depressing, to read a bad book by a writer one respects," she writes.[10] Jennifer Mattson of *Booklist* felt that the emphasis on vampires, among other themes, prevented Hinton from achieving her usual writing quality.[11] However, a reviewer writing in *Publishers Weekly* saw merit in *Hawkes Harbor* and called the book a "contemporary *Treasure Island* with a genre-bending twist."[12]

Hawkes Harbor allowed Hinton to relax and truly enjoy the writing process. Since she was writing in an entirely new genre, she did not feel as though she had to outdo herself with a book that was better than one of her previous books.[13] Because *Hawkes Harbor* contains mature themes, Hinton recommends it only for adults and not for her usual reading audience. "Don't buy it for your 12 year old," she advises.[14]

Chapter 9

"Just a Storyteller"

In a letter to S. E. Hinton, a young girl once wrote,

> Dear S.E. Hinton,
>
> When I was eleven years old, I read your book *The Outsiders* for the first time . . . When I was fourteen, my friend Joy passed away. I suddenly could understand what Ponyboy was feeling when his best friend Johnny died. . . . *The Outsiders* helped me through a difficult time in my life. It taught me that no matter what happens in life, there will always be hope for the future. I've read your book too many times to count, but I'll always remember the wonderful lessons that it taught me.[1]

Hinton has received thousands of such letters in the almost forty years since *The Outsiders* was published. They are a testament to the way she has changed young adult literature over the years. Hinton's books have helped young people face the reality of their lives, make decisions, and learn from their mistakes.

Hinton's books have also had an impact on how young people read. Her books have helped many reluctant readers come to know the pleasure of reading. Books like *The Outsiders* and *That Was Then, This Is Now* are found on the required reading lists of many middle and high schools. Often teachers begin reading the book in class with the students and then assign a chapter or two to be read at home for homework. Even those students who do not like to read find they cannot put the books down.[2]

Hinton has a theory for why this is so. "I think the readers identify with the characters so strongly. They either know somebody like that person or they feel they are just like that person. I get letters from kids saying, 'those aren't my problems, but those are my feelings,'" she explains.[3]

One of the reasons *The Outsiders* has remained popular with teen readers over the years is because of its timeless themes. Every generation has its share of teenagers who, like Ponyboy, Bryon, Rusty-James, and Hinton's other characters, feel misunderstood, unwanted, unloved, and confused. "Every teenager feels that adults have no idea what's going on. Even today the concept of the in-group and the out-group remains the same. The kids say, 'okay, this is like the Preppies and the Punks,' or whatever they call themselves.

The uniforms change, and the names of groups change, but kids really grasp how similar their situations are to Ponyboy's," Hinton explains.[4]

Hinton's groundbreaking writing also broke down barriers and opened doors for other young adult authors who also wished to write stories that did not always end in "happily ever after." Her writing paved the way for authors like Judy Blume, Paula Danziger, Robert Cormier, and a host of others to write realistic young adult fiction.

> **"I get letters from kids saying, 'those aren't my problems, but those are my feelings.'"**
>
> **—S.E. Hinton**

Over the years, fans have begged for a sequel to *The Outsiders*, and although Hinton knows she could make a "jillion"[5] dollars writing one, she knows she could no longer capture the "raw emotions" that made *The Outsiders* what it is today.[6]

"If I tried to write it now, when I'm a much better writer, I'd ruin it," she says. "[Readers] think I am being mean when I say, 'No, I won't write a sequel.' But I need to change that to, 'No, I CAN'T write a sequel,'" she says.[7]

Nearly forty years after the publication of *The Outsiders*, the book remains number-two on *Publishers Weekly*'s "All-Time Bestselling Children's Books" list. It ranks second only to *Charlotte's Web*.[8]

In 1998, Hinton's innovative approach to

writing for young people earned her a place in the Oklahoma Writers Hall of Fame. This award was established in 1991 to honor Oklahoma writers who have made major contributions to American literature while living and writing in Oklahoma. The writers are nominated by the general public and selected by a jury of writers who have already been inducted.[9]

"I'm just a storyteller," Hinton claimed in her acceptance speech. "If you put me in the hall of fame for my storytelling, then you might as well put me in for breathing because I can't help it."[10]

"I'm just a storyteller."

—S.E. Hinton

Hinton believes that as an author, she is but a messenger, and she would prefer that people focus on the messages found in her books rather than on her. The jacket covers of her books do not contain her picture and only rarely does she speak in public or give an interview. She and David, a software engineer, live a quiet life in Tulsa. Nick attends college. Both Hinton and David are introverts who enjoy spending time together at home.

Hinton's passion for horses has not diminished over the years and she is an avid horsewoman. She owns several horses and shows them. She also enjoys reading; to nourish her writing, she reads biographies because they are about character and "character drives my novels."[11] She also likes to

S.E. Hinton in attendance at the Oklahoma Writers Hall of Fame Award Banquet at the Philbrook Museum of Art in Tulsa, Oklahoma, on October 24, 1998.

read about history. She takes classes for fun at a nearby university and belongs to a weekly writers' group.

"People think I have been sitting here in an ivory tower with minions or something. But I've been wandering around the Safeway wondering what to cook for dinner like everybody else," Hinton told one interviewer.[12]

Hinton keeps her life as a writer separate from her other roles. Hinton explains it this way: "I'm not any one thing, and that's a reason I don't mind having a separate identity for my writing. I'm an author, but I'm also a mother, a friend, a horseback rider, a decent cook. Being involved

> **"I'm an author, but I'm also a mother, a friend, a horseback rider, a decent cook."**
>
> **—S.E. Hinton**

domestically keeps me in touch with reality. I don't mind having two identities; in fact, I like keeping the writer part separate in some ways."[13]

Hinton finds it hard to accept that the first book she ever wrote will be the one she is most remembered for.[14] "I see so many things wrong with it as a writer that I can't say that's the best writing I've ever done," she said.[15] Nevertheless, she realizes the impact her writing has had on young people and she is grateful. S.E. Hinton summarizes her life this way:

> I've been very lucky—I've written books that have had both critical and popular acclaim. I've been welcomed on movie sets where I have taken pride in leaving my "fingerprints" and made some life-long friends. I have a happy marriage and a great kid. I have been satisfied with some of my work, both published and not. But I always want the next work to be my best.[16]

And, says Hinton, if she ever forgets how it is to be a teenager in a savage social system, "I've got it all written down."[17]

In Her Own Words

The following section draws on several interviews with S.E. Hinton, including: one conducted by William Walsh, published in *From Writers to Students*; one conducted by Lisa Ehrichs in *Seventeen*; and interviews posted on the Random House Web site, S.E. Hinton's Web site, and in the back of *The Outsiders*.

On writing The Outsiders

While I was writing the book, I had no idea of plot structure—I still don't, I can't plot my way out of the Safeway store, but I know my characters. And, during the book, I would go so far as to say to my friends, "I'm writing a book; this is what's happened so far. What should happen next?" And they would tell me something, and I'd stick it in.

> —Walsh interview, *From Writers to Students: The Pleasures and Pains of Writing* (Newark, Del.: Scholastic, 1979).

I started writing [*The Outsiders*] before the women's movement was in full swing, and at the time, people wouldn't have believed that girls would do the things that I was writing about. I also felt more comfortable with the male point of view—I had grown up around boys.

—Ehrichs interview,
"Advice from a Penwoman,"
Seventeen, November 1981

I really enjoyed writing *The Outsiders* the most. I wasn't thinking about getting it published or what reviewers would think. I was just totally involved in the story. It's hard to do that when it is your profession.

—Official S.E. Hinton Web site
<http://www.sehinton.com>

[After *The Outsiders* was published] all the gang members I hung out with were sure they were in the book—but they aren't. I guess it's because these characters are really kind of universal without losing their identity.

—*The Outsiders*, (New York:
Puffin Books, 1997)

On using personal experience as a basis for plot

You mix up things that have happened to other people with your own experiences, and you take what your own experiences might have been and dramatize them into something completely different.

—Walsh interview

On writing Rumble Fish instead of a sequel to The Outsiders or That Was Then, This Is Now:

I enjoyed [writing *Rumble Fish*] because it was a challenge to me as a writer. It would have been very easy for me to write a sequel to *The Outsiders* or a sequel to *That Was Then* and go into *The Curtis Boys Visit the Farm* and that sort of thing, but I wanted to do something different and Rusty-James is different.

—Walsh interview

On advising young people who want to be writers:

Just do it! Don't think about it, don't agonize, sit down and write . . . . [D]o the best you possibly can. . . If you want to write better, you need to read better . . . Write, write, write, and read, read, read!

—Random House Web site, "Hang With the Authors: S.E. Hinton," Teens@Random, <http://www.randomhouse.com/teens/authors/ results.pperl?authorid=13074>

A lot of [young people] want to write and don't know where to begin. I always say that, first of all, they've got to read. Just read everything. . . . [R]eading lots of different styles will expose you to different ways of thinking. My big recommendation is to read and then practice. Write yourself. I wrote for eight years before I wrote *The Outsiders*. I advise writing for oneself. If you don't want to read it, nobody else is going to read it. Once you do that, and get somebody else's opinion, just send it out.

—Walsh interview

On the process of writing:

I don't really [have a particular writing habit].
I keep changing my methods, working around
other things in my life. *That Was Then, This Is
Now* was written in the two-pages-a-day method.
Rumble Fish was written on Thursday nights,
because that was when my husband played poker.
My fourth book, *Tex*, took me the longest to
write. I plotted it for three and a half years.
I wrote *Taming the Star Runner* on a schedule,
because 3 days a week [my son] Nick was in
preschool, and those were my writing days.
I guess my one technique throughout is to be
flexible about time and seize it when I can.

—Random House Web site

A novel gives you time to define characters, and
characters are my strong point. I think about
them until I know everything there is to know
about each of them.

—Ehrichs interview

I never studied writing consciously. But if you
read a lot, like I did, subconsciously, structure
is going to drop into your head, whether it's
sentence structure, paragraph structure, chapter
structure, or novel structure. Pretty soon, you're
going to know where things go—where the climax

is supposed to be, where the ending's supposed to be, how to get there, how to describe people. You can absorb it subconsciously. I, personally, never tried to copy any one person's style because I feel you should write the way you think.

—Walsh interview

I always begin with a character in mind and an ending I want to get to. I like my characters to grow, to show some change. So I know that in the middle of the book I'll have to figure out how to make the change happen. The middle is the hardest part for me.

—Random House Web site

Chronology

1950   S.E. Hinton is born, although her date of birth may actually be 1948.

1965   Hinton starts writing *The Outsiders*.

1966   Hinton graduates from Will Rogers High School in Tulsa, Oklahoma; she receives a contract to publish *The Outsiders*; she begins studies at University of Tulsa.

1967   *The Outsiders* is published; chosen as one of the *New York Herald Tribune*'s Best Teenage Books of 1967 and *Chicago Tribune*'s Book World Spring Book Festival Honor Book.

1968   Hinton's short story "Rumble Fish" is published in *Nimrod*.

1970   Hinton graduates from the University of Tulsa; she marries David Inhofe; they honeymoon in Spain.

1971   *That Was Then, This Is Now* is published and receives American Library Association Best Books for Young Adults award; also chosen as a *Chicago Tribune* Book World Spring Book Festival Honor Book.

1975   *The Outsiders* receives Media and Methods Maxi Award; named one of the Best Young Adult Books by the American Library Association; *Rumble Fish* is published and wins the American Library Association Best Book for Young Adults Award; *School Library Journal* names *Rumble Fish* one of the Best Books of the Year.

1978 *That Was Then, This Is Now* receives a Massachusetts Children's Book Award.

1979 *The Outsiders* receives Massachusetts Children's Book Award; *Tex* receives the American Library Association Best Books for Young Adults Award and a *School Library Journal* Best Book of the Year Award.

1980 *Tex* receives a New York Public Library "Book for the Teen-Age" citation.

1981 *Tex* receives an American Book Award Nomination.

1982 New Mexico Library Association gives *Rumble Fish* a "Land of Enchantment" Book Award; Louisiana Association of School Libraries awards *Tex* with a Sue Hefly Honor Book Award; *Tex* is nominated for the California Young Reader Medal by the California Reading Association; *Tex* is released as a movie by Disney Films.

1983 *The Outsiders* is made into a movie with Hinton cowriting the screenplay; son, Nicholas David Inhofe, is born; the movie version of *Rumble Fish* is released; Hinton receives a Golden Archer Award from the students of Wisconsin; *Tex* receives a Sue Hefly Award from the Louisiana Association of School Librarians.

1985 *That Was Then, This Is Now* is released as a movie; *The Outsiders* is adapted for television.

1988 Hinton is awarded the first Margaret A. Edwards Lifetime Achievement Award by American Library Association's Young Adult Services Division and School Library Journal; *Taming the Star Runner* is published and is named an American Library Association Best Book for Young Adults.

1989 *Taming the Star Runner* is named an American Library Association Quick Pick Book for Reluctant Young Adult Readers.

1995 *Big David, Little David* and *The Puppy Sister* are published; *The Puppy Sister* is awarded the Parents' Choice Silver Honor Book.

1997 Hinton wins the Arrell Gibson Lifetime Achievement Award from Oklahoma Center for the Book.

1998 Hinton is inducted into the Oklahoma Writers Hall of Fame.

2004 *Hawkes Harbor* is published.

2005 *The Outsiders* movie, produced by Francis Ford Coppola, is re-released as a DVD.

2006 Two new paperback editions of *The Outsiders* are released in April and May.

2007 *The Outsiders* celebrates its fortieth anniversary of publication.

Chapter Notes

Chapter 1. "The Voice of the Youth"

1. "Susan Eloise Hinton," *Contemporary Authors Online*, 2005, <http://infotrac.galegroup.com> (February 1, 2006).

2. S.E. Hinton, "Teenagers Are for Real," *The New York Times Book Review*, August 27, 1967, pp. 26–29.

3. Veronica Loveday, "S.E. Hinton," *Arts and Entertainment: American Literature, 2000*, <http://search.epnet.com> (April 1, 2006).

4. Jay Daly, *Presenting S.E. Hinton* (Boston: Twayne, 1987), p. 1.

5. Ibid., preface.

6. Jerry M. Weiss, ed., *From Writers to Students: The Pleasures and Pains of Writing*, IRA Literature for Adolescence Committee (Newark, Del.: IRA Association, 1979), p. 32.

7. "About S.E. Hinton," n.d., <http://www.mrcoward.com/slcusd/sehi.html> (March 25, 2006).

8. "S.E. Hinton," *Authors and Artists for Young Adults* (Detroit: Thomson Gale, 2001), p. 65.

9. Lillian Gerhardt, *School Library Journal*, May 15, 1967, p. 136.

10. Loveday, "S.E. Hinton."

11. "S.E. Hinton: Penguin U.K. Authors," March 3, 2003, <http://www.penguin.co.uk/nf/Author/AuthorPage/0,,1000015109,00.html> (April 14, 2006).

12. Michael Malone, "Tough Puppies," *Nation*, March 8, 1986, p. 276.

13. Susan Hinton, "Teenagers Are for Real," *The New York Times*, August 27, 1967, pp. BR-14.

14. *"Tex* and Other Teen Tales," *Something About the Author* (Detroit: Gale Research Inc., 1990), p. 98.

15. Thomas Fleming, "Review of *The Outsiders*," *The New York Times Book Review*, May 1967, part 2, pp. 10–12.

16. Jane Manthorne, "Review of *The Outsiders*," *Horn Book*, August 1967, p. 475, in *Contemporary Authors Online*.

17. "S.E. Hinton: Penguin U.K. Authors."

18. "Susan Eloise Hinton," *Contemporary Authors Online*.

Chapter 2. "A Teenage Wonder"

1. Dinitia Smith, "An Outsider, Out of the Shadows; With the Release of a Recut 'Outsiders,' a Secretive Author Is Willing to Talk," *The New York Times*, September 7, 2005, p. E1.

2. S.E. Hinton, "Children's Author/Illustrator Biographies: Autobiographical Statement," *Educational Paperback Association*, n.d., <http://www.edupaperback.org/showauth2.cfm?authid=81> (October 17, 2006).

3. Adam Langer, "Where Are They Now?" *Book*, July/August 2003, p. 36.

4. Personal e-mail correspondence with Dr. M.A. Brown, April 2006.

5. Smith.

6. Laurie Lanzen Harris, ed., *Biography Today: Profiles of People of Interest to Young Readers* (Holmes, Pa.: Omnigraphics, 1995), p. 76.

7. "Hang With the Authors: S.E. Hinton," *Teens@Random*, n.d., <http://www.random-house.com/teens/authors/results.pperl?authorid= 13074> (March 26, 2006).

8. Jay Daly, *Presenting S.E. Hinton* (Boston: Twayne Publishers, 1989), p. 3.

9. Smith.

10. Doris De Montreville and Elizabeth Crawford, eds., *Fourth Book of Junior Authors* (H.W. Wilson, 1978).

11. Don Swaim, "Wired for Books: Audio Interview With S.E. Hinton," 1987, <http://wiredforbooks. org/sehinton/> (May 1, 2006).

12. "Speaking With S.E. Hinton," *The Outsiders Movie and Book Site*, <http://www. theoutsidersbookandmovie.com/TheBook.html> (April 14, 2006).

13. Daly.

14. Ibid., p. 4.

15. Doris De Montreville and Elizabeth Crawford, eds., *Fourth Book of Junior Authors*, in *Something About the Author* (Detroit: Gale, 1990), vol. 58, p. 90.

16. Swaim.

17. Smith.

18. Ibid.

19. Ibid.

20. "Face to Face With a Teen-Age Novelist," *Seventeen*, October 1967, in *Something About the Author* (Detroit: Gale, 1980), vol. 19, p. 148.

21. Personal e-mail interview with Douglass E. McCracken, April 17, 2006.

22. Lisa Ehrichs, "Advice from a Penwoman," *Seventeen*, vol. 40, November 1981, p. 32.

23. Stephen Farber, "Directors Join the S.E. Hinton Fan Club," *The New York Times*, March 20, 1983, p. 2.

24. "S.E. Hinton: On Writing *Tex*," notes from Delacorte Press for Books for Young Readers, Winter 1979/Spring 1980, S.E. Hinton Teacher Resource File, n.d., <http://falcon.jmu.edu/~ramseyil/hinton.htm> (March 21, 2006).

25. Daly, p. 2.

26. Swaim.

27. Carol Wallace, "In Praise of Teenage Outcasts," *Daily News*, September 26, 1982.

28. Swaim.

29. "Face to Face With a Teen-Age Novelist," *Seventeen*, October 1967, in *Something About the Author*, vol. 58, p. 98.

30. Jerry M. Weiss, ed., *From Writers to Students: The Pleasures and Pains of Writing* (Newark, Del.: International Reading Association, 1979), p. 32.

31. "Face to Face With a Teen-Age Novelist," *Something About the Author*, vol. 58, p. 98.

32. Susan Hinton, "Teenagers are for Real," *The New York Times Book Review*, August 27, 1967.

33. Ibid.

34. Yvonne Litchfield, "Her Book to Be Published Soon, But Tulsa Teen-Ager Keeps Cool," *Tulsa Daily World*, quoted in *Contemporary Authors Online*, Thomson Gale, 2005.

35. Karen Valby, "Open Range," *Entertainment Weekly*, September 10, 2004, p. 169.

Chapter 3. As Good as Gold

1. S.E. Hinton, *The Outsiders* (New York: Puffin Books, 1997).

2. *"The Outsiders* by S. E. Hinton—Summaries and Commentaries—Chapter 5," *Yahoo! Education*, n.d., <http://education.yahoo.com/homework_help/cliffsnotes/the_outsiders/19.html> (March 23, 2007).

3. S.E. Hinton, *The Outsiders*.

4. Jerry M. Weiss, ed., *From Writers to Students: The Pleasures and Pains of Writing* (Newark, Del.: International Reading Association, 1979), p. 32.

5. Ibid.

6. "Face to Face With a Teen-Age Novelist," *Something About the Author*, vol. 58, p. 98.

7. Ibid.

8. Geoff Fox, *Twentieth-Century Children's Writers*, D.L. Kirkpatrick, ed. (New York: St. Martin's Press, 1983), p. 377.

9. "A Conversation With S.E. Hinton," *Penguin Academics Authors*, n.d., <http://academics.penguin.co.uk/nf/Author/AuthorPage/> (March 26, 2006).

10. Judy Randle, "Inside *The Outsiders*: Hinton to Be Inducted into Hall of Fame," *Language Arts*, n.d., <http://ecuip.lib.uchicago.edu/dilib/language/outsiders/halloffame.html> (March 26, 2006).

11. Lillian Gerhardt, *School Library Journal*, May 15, 1967, p. 136.

12. Nat Hentoff, "Review of *The Outsiders*," *Atlantic Monthly*, December 1967.

13. Unidentified reviewer, "On the Hook," *The Times Literary*, October 30, 1970, p. 1258.

14. "Susan Eloise Hinton," *Contemporary Authors Online*, 2005, <http://infotrac.galegroup.com> (February 1, 2006).

15. Daly, p. 17.

16. Ibid, p. 18.

17. Ibid.

18. *S.E. Hinton Teacher Resource File*, n.d., <http://falcon.jmu.edu/~ramseyil/hinton.htm> (March 21, 2006).

19. Weiss, p. 34.

20. Daly, p. 97.

21. Susan Hinton, "Teenagers are for Real," *The New York Times Book Review*, August 27, 1967.

22. Ibid.

23. S.E. Hinton audio interview with Don Swaim, 1987, <http://wiredforbooks.org> (May 1, 2006).

24. Lisa Ehrichs, "Advice from a Penwoman," *Seventeen*, vol. 40, November 1981, p. 32.

25. American Library Association Web site, 2006, <http://www.ala.org> (May 1, 2006).

26. "Banned Books Week," *American Booksellers Web site*, n.d., <http://www.abffe.org/bbw-booklist-detailed.htm> (May 1, 2006).

27. Susan Eloise Hinton," *Contemporary Authors Online*, 2005, <http://infotrac.galegroup.com> (February 1, 2006).

28. Gerhardt.

29. Zena Sutherland, "The Teen-Ager Speaks," *The Saturday Review*, January 27, 1968, p. 34.

30. Ibid.

31. Jay Daly, p. 67.

Chapter 4. "Growth Is Betrayal"

1. Lisa Ehrichs, "Advice from a Penwoman," *Seventeen*, vol. 40, November 1981, p. 32.
2. Ibid.
3. Jerry M. Weiss, ed., *From Writers to Students: The Pleasures and Pains of Writing* (Newark, Del.: International Reading Association, 1979), p. 32.
4. Laurie Lanzen Harris, ed., *Biography Today: Profiles of People of Interest to Young Readers* (Holmes, Pa.: Omnigraphics, 1995), p. 76.
5. Brian Heater, "Staying Golden," *New York Press*, n.d., <http://www.nypress.com/17/38/books/BrianHeater/cfm> (May 22, 2006).
6. *"Rumble Fish," Teens@Random*, n.d., <http://www.randomhouse.com/teens/catalog/display.pperl?isbn=9780440975342> (January 3, 2007).
7. Jay Daly, *Presenting S.E. Hinton* (Boston: Twayne, 1987), p. 39.
8. S.E. Hinton, *That Was Then, This Is Now* (New York: Puffin Books, 1998).
9. Weiss, p. 35.
10. Sheryl Andrews, "Review of *That Was Then, This Is Now*," *Horn Book*, July/August 1971, p. 338.
11. "Biography," *Official S.E. Hinton Web site*, n.d., <http://www.sehinton.com/bio/index.html> (March 26, 2006).
12. Michael Cart, "Review of *That Was Then, This Is Now*," *The New York Times Book Review*, August 8, 1971, p. 338.
13. Daly, p. 59.

Chapter 5. Brotherly Love

1. S.E. Hinton, *Rumble Fish* (New York: Delacorte, 1975), p. 5.

2. Ibid.

3. Linda Plemons, "Author Laureate of Adolescent Fiction," *University of Tulsa Annual*, 1983–1984, pp. 62–71.

4. *Rumble Fish* production notes, quoted in Commire, *Something About the Author*, vol. 58 (Detroit: Gale Research, Inc., 1990), pp. 98–104.

5. Ibid.

6. Ibid.

7. "Susan Eloise Hinton," *Contemporary Authors Online*, 2005, <http://infotrac.galegroup.com> (February 1, 2006).

8. Jay Daly, *Presenting S.E. Hinton* (Boston: Twayne, 1987), p. 41.

9. "Susan Eloise Hinton," *Contemporary Authors Online*.

10. Jerry M. Weiss, ed., *From Writers to Students: The Pleasures and Pains of Writing* (Newark, Del.: International Reading Association, 1979), p. 122.

11. Ibid.

12. Daly, p. 98.

13. Margery Fisher, "Review of *Rumble Fish*," *Growing Point*, May 1976, quoted in *Contemporary Authors Online*.

14. "Review of *Rumble Fish*," *Publishers Weekly*, July 28, 1975, p. 122.

15. Jane Abramson, "Review of *Rumble Fish*," *School Library Journal*, October 1975, p. 106.

16. Anita Silvey, "Review of *Rumble Fish*," *Horn Book Magazine*, November/December 1975, p. 601.

17. Robert Berkvist, "Review of *Rumble Fish*," *The New York Times Book Review*, December 14, 1975, p. 8.

18. Stephen Farber, "Directors Join the S.E. Hinton Fan Club," *The New York Times*, March 20, 1983, p. 2.

19. Ibid.

20. Daly, p. 87.

21. *Official S.E. Hinton Web site*, n.d., <http://www.s.e.hinton.com/> (February 22, 2006).

22. Gene Lyons, "On Tulsa's Mean Streets," *Newsweek*, October 11, 1982, p. 105.

23. *Official S.E. Hinton Web site*.

24. S.E. Hinton, *Tex* (New York: Delacorte, 1979).

25. "Notes from Delacorte Press for Books for Young Readers," *S.E. Hinton Teacher Resource File*, n.d., <http://falcon.jmu.edu/~ramseyil/hinton.htm> (March 21, 2006).

26. Ibid.

27. Ibid.

28. Ibid.

29. Marilyn Kaye, "Review of *Tex*," *School Library Journal*, November 15, 1979, p. 88.

30. Daly, p. 94.

31. Margery Fisher, "Review of *Tex*," *Growing Points*, May 1980, pp. 3686–3687, quoted in *Contemporary Authors Online*.

32. Paxton Davis, "Review of *Tex*," *The New York Times Book Review*, December 16, 1979, p. 23.

33. Lance Salway, "Review of *Tex*," *Signal*, May 1980, pp. 120–122.

34. Stephen Farber, "Directors Join the S.E. Hinton Fan Club," *The New York Times*, March 20, 1983, p. 2.

35. Ibid.

Chapter 6. *Taming the Star Runner*

1. "Susan Eloise Hinton," *Contemporary Authors Online*, 2005, <http://infotrac.galegroup.com> (February 1, 2006).

2. *"Taming the Star Runner," Teens@Random*, n.d., <http://www.randomhouse.com/teens/catalog/display.pperl?isbn=9780440204794> (March 26, 2006).

3. S.E. Hinton, *Taming the Star Runner* (New York: Delacorte Press, 1988).

4. *"Taming the Star Runner," Teens@Random*.

5. Jerry M. Weiss, ed., *From Writers to Students: The Pleasures and Pains of Writing*, (Newark, Del.: International Reading Association, 1979), p. 32.

6. Ibid.

7. Ibid.

8. *Official S.E. Hinton Web site*, n.d., <http://www.sehinton.com> (February 22, 2006).

9. Charlene Strickland, "A Review of *Taming the Star Runner*," *School Library Journal*, vol. 35, issue 2, October 1988, p. 161.

10. Nancy Vasilakis, "Review of *Taming the Star Runner*," *Horn Book*, January/February 1989, pp. 78–79.

11. Patty Campbell, "Review of *Taming the Star Runner*," *The New York Times Book Review*, April 2, 1989, p. 37.

12. Jay Daly, as quoted in "Susan Eloise Hinton," *Contemporary Authors Online*, 2005, <http://infotrac.galegroup.com> (February 1, 2006).

13. "Review of *Taming the Star Runner*," *Kirkus Reviews*, September 15, 1988, p. 1241.

14. Adam Langer, "Where Are They Now?" *Book*, July/August 2003, p. 34.

Chapter 7. Kids and Puppies

1. Patty Campbell, "Review of *Taming the Star Runner*," *The New York Times Book Review*, April 2, 1989, p. 37.

2. Dave Smith, "Hinton, What Boys Are Made Of," *Los Angeles Times*, July 15, 1982, quoted in "S.E. Hinton," *Contemporary Authors Online*, 2005, <http://infotrac.galegroup.com> (February 1, 2006).

3. "Inside the Outsider: Susie Loves Matt," *Language Arts*, n.d., <http://ecuip.lib.uchicago. edu/diglib/language/outsiders/movie.html> (February 1, 2006).

4. "Author Profile: S.E. Hinton," *Bookreporter.com*, October 8, 2004, <http://bookreporter.com/ authors/au-hinton-se.asp> (April 23, 2006).

5. S.E. Hinton, *Big David, Little David* (New York: Doubleday, 1995).

6. Jody McCoy, "Book Review: Preschool and Primary Grades—*The Puppy Sister*," *School Library Journal*, vol. 41, issue 10, October 1995, p. 104.

7. Carolyn Phelen, "Books for Youth: Books for the Young—*Big David, Little David*," *Booklist*, vol. 91, January 15, 1995. p. 936.

8. Elizabeth Devereux, and Diane Roback, "Forecasts: Children's Books-Review of *Big David, Little David*," *Publishers Weekly*, vol. 241, December 12, 1994, p. 62.

9. "Frequently Asked Questions," *The Official S.E. Hinton Web site*, n.d., <http://www.sehinton. com> (April 21, 2006).

10. "*Rumble Fish*," *Teens@Random*, n.d., <http:// www.randomhouse.com/teens/catalog/display. pperl?isbn=9780440975342> (April 21, 2006).

11. Ibid.

12. "About the Author," *Random House Web site*, <http://www.randomhouse.com/author> (April 21, 2006).

13. S.E. Hinton, *The Puppy Sister* (New York: Delacorte, 1995).

14. *"Taming the Star Runner," Teens@Random*, n.d., <http://www.randomhouse.com/teens/catalog/ display.pperl?isbn=9780440204794> (April 21, 2006).

15. Susanna Rodell, "A Review of *The Puppy Sister*," *The New York Times Book Review*, November 19, 1995, p. 37.

16. Unnamed reviewer, "Review of *The Puppy Sister*," *Publishers Weekly*, July 17, 1995, p. 230.

17. Jody McCoy, "Book Review: Preschool and Primary Grades—*The Puppy Sister*," *School Library Journal*, vol. 41, April 1995, p. 104.

Chapter 8. *Hawkes Harbor*

1. "Author Profile: S.E. Hinton," *Bookreporter.com*, October 8, 2004, <http://bookreporter.com/ authors/au-hinton-se.asp> (April 23, 2006).

2. S.E. Hinton, *Hawkes Harbor* (New York: Tor, 2004).

3. Karen Valby, "Open Range," *Entertainment Weekly*, September 10, 2004, p. 169.

4. *Official Web site of S.E. Hinton*, n.d., <http:// www.sehinton.com> (April 21, 2006).

5. Marrit Ingman, "Don't Buy It for Your 12-Year-Old," *The Austin Chronicle*, October 29, 2004, <http://www.austinchronicle.com/gyrobase/Issue /story? oid=oid%3A235104> (April 21, 2006).

6. *Official S.E. Hinton Web site*.

7. Valby.

8. Ingman.

9. Ibid.

10. Elizabeth Hand, "The Lost Boys," *Washington Post*, December 12, 2004, p. T05.

11. Jennifer Mattson, "Review of *Hawkes Harbor*," *Booklist*, August 1994, p. 1871.

12. Unnamed reviewer, "Review of *Hawkes Harbor*," *Publishers Weekly*, August 9, 2004, p. 230.

13. Kelly Kurt, "S.E. Hinton Breaks Free with Adult Book," *Oakland Tribune*, September 26, 2004, <http://findarticles.com/p/articles/mi_qn4176/ is_20040926/ai n14586041> (May 22, 2006).

14. Ingman.

Chapter 9. "Just a Storyteller"

1. Lois Lowry, ed., *Dear Author* (Berkeley: Weekly Reader, 1995), p. 30.

2. Lisa Rubin, "The Young and the Restless," *Media and Methods*, May/June, 1982 quoted in *Something About the Author* (Detroit: Gale Research Inc., 1990), p. 101.

3. Ibid.

4. "Speaking with S.E. Hinton," *The Outsiders Movie and Book Site*, <http://www. theoutsidersbookandmovie.com/TheBook.html> (April 14, 2006).

5. Karen Valby, "Open Range," *Entertainment Weekly*, September 10, 2004, p. 169.

6. Kelly Kurt, "S.E. Hinton Breaks Free with Adult Book," *Oakland Tribune*, September 26, 2004, <http://findarticles.com/p/articles/mi_qn4176/ is_20040926/ai_n14586041> (May 22, 2006).

7. Ibid.

8. "Author Profile: S.E. Hinton," *Bookreporter.com*, October 8, 2004, <http://bookreporter.com/authors/au-hinton-se.asp> (April 23, 2006).

9. "The Oklahoma Writers Hall of Fame," *Oklahoma Center for Poets and Writers Web site*, n.d., <http://poetsandwriters.okstate.edu/halloffame/index.html> (April 26, 2006).

10. Ibid.

11. "Hang With the Authors: S.E. Hinton," *Teens@Random*, n.d., <http://www.random-house.com/teens/authors/results.pperl?authorid=13074> (March 26, 2006).

12. Adam Langer, "Where Are They Now?" *Book*, July/August 2003, p. 34.

13. "Hang With the Authors: S.E. Hinton."

14. S.E. Hinton audio interview with Don Swaim, 1987, <http://wiredforbooks.org> (May 1, 2006).

15. Jerry M. Weiss, ed., *From Writers to Students: The Pleasures and Pains of Writing*. (Newark, Del.: International Reading Association, 1979), p. 32.

16. "10 Questions: S.E.Hinton," *IGN.com*, July 6, 2004, <http://filmforce.ign.com/articles/527/527689p1.html> (January 3, 2007).

17. Quoted in Ann Commire, *Something About the Author* (Detroit: Gale Research Inc., 1980), p. 148.

Glossary

articulate—Well-spoken.

blue-collar worker—A member of the working class who performs manual labor.

fluke—Something good that happens by accident.

idealism—The pursuit of high goals.

Galahad—A chivalrous man; someone who takes after Sir Galahad, one of King Arthur's Knights.

new money—Money recently earned or acquired.

protagonist—The leading character in a book, play, or movie.

realism—Recognizing circumstances as they are.

retrospective—Looking backward.

Trail of Tears—The route the Cherokee Indians were forced to travel after they were displaced from their homes in Georgia and relocated in Oklahoma.

Major Works by S.E. Hinton

Further Reading

Books

Daly, Jay. *Presenting S.E. Hinton*. Boston: Twayne, 1987.

Drew, Bernard A. *The 100 Most Popular Young Adult Authors*. Portsmouth, N.H.: Libraries Unlimited, 1997.

Wilson, Antoine. *S. E. Hinton*. New York: Rosen Publishing Group, 2003.

Internet Addresses

S.E. Hinton Official Web Site
http://www.sehinton.com/

The Outsiders Official Movie and Book Site
http://www.theoutsidersbookandmovie.com

Oklahoma Center for Poets and Writers
http://poetsandwriters.okstate.edu/halloffame/schinton.html

Index